WARREN BUFFETT

Abha Sharma is an author, a novelist, a personality development trainer and a life coach. Her books include the novel *The Night of Fear* and motivational books *The Making of the Greatest: Jack Ma* and *The Making of the Greatest: Mark Zuckerberg*. She is a qualified university-level educator and has worked extensively with international industry leaders in online education and with prestigious higher education institutions. She has a deep interest in the mysteries of existence and draws upon her observations as a life coach, especially human behaviour in the face of challenges. With an immense faith in the human potential, she believes in continued learning.

Know more about her at:
LinkedIn: www.linkedin.com/in/abha-sharma-a1774a169/
Twitter: @abha_e

Also by the author:

The Night of Fear
The Making of the Greatest: Jack Ma
The Making of the Greatest: Mark Zuckerberg

THE MAKING OF THE GREATEST
WARREN BUFFETT

Abha Sharma

RUPA

Published by
Rupa Publications India Pvt. Ltd 2021
7/16, Ansari Road, Daryaganj
New Delhi 110002

Sales centres:
Prayagraj Bengaluru Chennai
Hyderabad Jaipur Kathmandu
Kolkata Mumbai

P-ISBN: 978-93-90918-35-5
E-ISBN: 978-93-90918-36-2

Fourth impression 2023

10 9 8 7 6 5 4

The moral right of the author has been asserted.

Printed in India

CONTENTS

CONTENTS

INTRODUCTION

An eager audience at the University of Nebraska looks on as a man in his 70s, wearing an inconspicuous-looking suit takes to the stage. With his smile and unassuming body language, he looks approachable, yet there is an aura of significance about him. He taps on the mike and with a hint of playfulness, says, 'Testing...one million...two million...three million.' The audience roars in appreciative laughter, knowing fully well that millions and billions of dollars is what he deals in. He begins his speech with modest words, but every word he utters and every grain of advice he gives is lapped up eagerly not just by the room full of students but also by the big shots striking gigantic deals on Wall Street. When this man shares his ideas, people in the financial world put everything else on hold.

Warren Edward Buffett—legendary investor, one of the world's richest men, the oracle of Omaha, the wizard of the stock market, the most successful investor in the world, philanthropist, business magnate and the most frugal mega-billionaire. He is even known as Warren 'Bailout' Buffett for his capacity to bail out seriously large organizations like national banks and airlines out of deep financial trouble. Think of money in the modern world and you think of Warren Buffett. From earning a profit of two cents selling chewing gum at the age of six, Buffett has built a net worth of approximately $88.5 billion (as of 13 January 2021). The list of his achievements is a long one, but to mention a few, he is one of the wealthiest people in the world. In 2008, *Forbes* named him the richest person in the world. He has been named the top money manager of the twentieth century. In 2007, he was on the *Time* list of the hundred most influential people. A tax plan in the United States, the 'Buffett Rule' is named after him. He runs Berkshire Hathaway, one of the world's largest public companies, with a market capitalization of more than $500 billion. A two-hour dinner meeting with him costs more than $4.5 million, though the entire money goes to charity.

Thus, it is not surprising that Buffett's popular image is coloured in shades of dollar bills. He is thought of as a money-making machine, with supernatural powers to take the most rewarding decisions in the stock market. He is generally perceived as a person with a magical formula for growing money, one who has pursued no other interest in life other than increasing his pile of money, and simultaneously, has helped other people increase their wealth exponentially. Since 1965, Buffett's company Berkshire Hathaway has produced an average growth in book value at an incredible 19 per cent for its shareholders.

Keeping all the financial superlatives aside, what Buffett has earned for himself is quintessential respect. How many people manage to get super rich by keeping faith on their judgement and without compromising on their values? Buffett is an epitome of the surreal financial superman who gathered riches, yet maintained strong ethics and retained the childlike curiosity to learn forever. The respect he arouses in people is as much for his strong value system as it is for the empire he has built. He also generates curiosity because his quest for money was not for the wealth itself, for he stays away from most luxuries and has an extremely simple lifestyle. He never spent an extra penny, yet he has pledged to donate 99 per cent of his wealth to charity.

The magic that Buffett spins is a result of a lifetime of consistent efforts and ceaseless learning. Every stage in the man's life was a step towards the pinnacle. A peek into Buffett's journey would give an understanding of the man and the legacy he has created.

CHILDHOOD

I t is interesting that Buffett was born at a time when the most prominent topic in America was money, or rather the lack of it—1930. America was in the midst of its worst-ever economic setback, the Great Depression. Beginning with the Wall Street crash of October 1929, the country was facing an unprecedented crisis. Poverty, unemployment and loss of trust were widespread. During those troubled times, one of the best-known investors of all times, Warren Edward Buffett was born on 30 August 1930 to Howard Buffett and Leila Stahl Buffett of Omaha, Nebraska.

Warren's father, Howard Buffett, is best remembered as a politician from Nebraska. However, before becoming a politician, he was a major in journalism and had begun his career as a stockbroker with the Union

State Bank. But just a couple of years into his career, the stock market crashed, and he lost his job as well as his money, as banks closed one after the other. At that time, he had two young children, three-year-old Doris and a year-old Warren, and a wife to take care of. After failing to get a job, he started his own stockbrokerage firm with two partners.

Howard managed to steadily grow his business and give his family a comfortable life. All this while his interest in politics as well as his inclination towards the Republican Party were growing. Consequently, he ran for the US House of Representatives in 1942 and was elected. He got re-elected twice after that, in 1945 and 1949. Howard Buffett is known for his strict ethical principles, one demonstration of which is his refusal to accept a salary hike of $2,500 while he was in office because he had been elected on a lower salary. He was also a vocal advocate of the supreme importance of human liberty. Howard's personality had a long-lasting impact on young Warren. The portrait of his father in Warren's office is a symbolic representation of this lasting influence.

Warren Buffett's mother, Leila, took care of her home and children, enthusiastically helped her husband in his career and was perceived a socially pleasant person, but she had an unspecified psychological problem that confused Doris, Warren and their younger sister, Roberta. Leila was her normal self in social interactions, but often with her children, she tended to have a 'temper'. Her bouts of anger were directed at her three children, with the trigger always being something related to them. The undiagnosed psychological condition that Leila had led to a tense family environment. Three-year-old Warren and five-year-old Doris were afraid of their mother's anger and tried to maintain a distance. They felt safer with their father. When the family sat down together, the discussions were mostly about money, investments or politics but hardly ever about emotional needs.

Leila's temper had the most adverse effect on Doris, but Warren found out ways to escape this unpleasantness in his mother's presence. He diverted himself with things that kept him busy, spending most of his after-school time with the kids in the neighbourhood or at certain relatives' homes. He particularly liked to spend time with his aunt Alice, his father's sister, from whom he got love and warmth, and more importantly, she took an active interest in Warren's activities. She often laid out conditions for him, tricking him to eat healthy things such as broccoli in return for gifts.

While Alice's presence filled the gap of maternal warmth in Warren's life, another person who had a great impact on the little child was his paternal grandfather, Ernest Buffett. Ernest ran a grocery store and was a popular figure in Omaha. He was always careful with money and knew how to run his business in difficult times. He was thrifty and practical and dealt with his employees with a certain tightfistedness but was loved by his grandchildren. Warren imbibed much from him, and even as a child, keenly observed the way his grandfather ran his business.

The Child in Love with Numbers

Warren Buffett loves numbers. He can perform gigantic calculations in his mind, reportedly does not use a calculator and can rattle off figures and numbers with ease. Interestingly, his passion for numbers began as early as his preschool days. Numbers fascinated him in every form and he was observant about patterns in which alphabets and numbers were arranged. One of the activities he enjoyed was observing the licence plates of cars. He and one of his friends, Bob Russel, would sit outside the latter's home, meticulously noting down the registration numbers of the passing cars. They did this for hours, and Warren later liked to figure out the frequency with which alphabets and numbers appeared on the plates. Both the kids secretly treated this as a spy game. At other times, the kids spread out the local newspaper, and tried to find out which letters appeared most frequently on the pages.

Simultaneous with his observation of numbers, reading also grew to be one of his passions. He loved reading, particularly books, but his reading had an additional dimension to it. He spent a lot of time observing the pages of books, including the Bible, trying to figure out which letters appeared the most. Clearly, he had a knack for observing patterns and their frequency.

Another one of Warren's favourite activities was maintaining a collection of soda bottle caps from around the town, especially from filing stations. While this may have been a child's simple pastime, for Warren, it meant much more. He meticulously rearranged the caps and observed which soda brand's caps were the most in number. At this young age, he could figure out that people apparently loved a particular soda more than the others. He enjoyed the thought that he had access to some information that other people around were simply overlooking. The possession of such 'secret' knowledge fascinated him.

A gift from Aunt Alice turned out to be a revelation of the child's analytical mind. This was a stopwatch and Warren was fascinated by its working and its ability to record with precision. He designed a game in which he, along with his sisters or friends, dropped marbles into a bathtub filled with water. As the marbles raced down the gentle slope towards the drain, he used the stopwatch to record the time each marble took. The fun part of this game was not everything; Warren was trying to observe a pattern, some probability that depended on specific conditions. The analytical mind was already in action.

Early Education

As he started attending Rose Hill Elementary School, Warren maintained a coin collection and a stamp collection in addition to the soda bottle caps. Observing, segregating and re-arranging seemed to fascinate him. While he was in second grade, he got to do his favourite thing—solving arithmetic problems on a blackboard. Though the problems were of simple addition, subtraction, division and multiplication, Warren seemed to take immense pleasure in competing over these with the other students. He often turned out to be the winner, never getting tired of working with numbers. Competitiveness, in fact, was one of his earliest visible traits. He enjoyed having various playful competitions with the other children in his class and in his neighbourhood.

By this time, he had started getting a clear understanding that he didn't really enjoy physical activity. His competitions were more in the intellectual domain rather than in sports. He tried boxing and skating but didn't follow up. However, he did play a little basketball and enjoyed ping-pong (or what we call table-tennis). He had numerous competitions with family and friends on the ping-pong table installed at his home. In addition, he learnt to play the cornet, which is similar to a trumpet, and even participated in a school event as a cornet player.

Warren's love of numbers grew with time. In fifth grade, he had literally learnt the population of every city listed in the 1939 *World Almanac*. The latter was a bestselling reference book that mentioned various facts about the world. Warren loved this book, and again, he went into analysis mode, figuring out which of the cities had a population of more than a million. He repeated the feat when his grandfather bought him a book about baseball. He absorbed every bit of detail about the players and their teams mentioned in the book. A book on bridges, a gift from Aunt Alice, caught his fancy, and generated his interest in a game that has probably played a role in his analytical thinking to this date.

As Warren grew up, he got increasingly interested in money, and more so in the methods by which it could be earned. This thought was probably a constant companion as he attended school, played with the kids in his neighbourhood and interacted with the adults in his life, like any other child of his age. Unlike many other parents, his were not bothered if they observed their six-year-old thinking of ways to make money. While Warren's father was a stockbroker himself, his mother was reportedly good with numbers too. The other close relative, Aunt Alice, was a home economics teacher. Most of all, his grandfather, Ernest Buffett, seemed to like the idea of little children getting interested in earning money. Thus, facilitated by his environment,

Warren started getting increasingly inquisitive about the way money worked. The thought process had begun.

CHILDHOOD

Warren started getting increasingly inquisitive about the way money worked. The thought process had begun.

STARTING YOUNG, REALLY YOUNG

As Warren grew up, so did his interest in monetary matters. His education apparently was not limited to school; he was constantly educating himself about the process of earning money. Quite incredible as it may sound for a child from a reasonably good financial background, Warren earned money for the first time when he was barely six years old. The 'business' was selling chewing gum packs. He bought different flavours of gum in packs from his grandfather's grocery shop, and in the evenings, he sold them to people in his neighbourhood.

What makes this story even more interesting is that this six-year-old could quickly do a mental calculation to avoid running into a loss. A particular incident illustrates this well. Warren vended each pack of five gums for five cents, making a profit of two cents per pack. A lady once wanted to buy just one piece out of the pack. Warren refused, quickly calculating in his mind that if he sold a single piece, he would have to sell the remaining four pieces as singles too, and he didn't think it was worth the effort and time.

During the summers, Warren took to selling Coca-Cola. He found it more profitable than selling chewing gum as selling Coca-Cola brought him a profit of five cents for every six bottles. At an age when most children struggle with the basics of mathematics, Warren could clearly work out the numbers and see which activity made more business sense. The reward of his hard work was money in the form of coins. He collected his earnings in a drawer at home and took great interest in arranging the coins systematically. While at work, he felt proud of wearing a money changer on his belt. It was a nickel-coated coin organizer gifted to him by one of his aunts. It made it easy for him to keep coins of different denominations. The belt was almost symbolic of the 'professionalism' that the child felt while doing this work.

Soon, Warren started door-to-door sale of newspapers. He sold Saturday *Evening Post* and *Liberty* magazine. He made a profit of one cent per paper and delivered around 500 papers a day. Though that seemed like a small amount, for Warren, it meant an important addition to his savings. The child had somehow imbibed the importance of having some cash around, and whenever possible, to grow that treasure. In other words, Warren had learnt the importance of earning money and of growing richer when he was not even 10 years old.

Warren was working fine with his little odd jobs, but the child still had to learn the right and the wrong ways of earning money. When he was around nine years old, he picked up used golf balls and sold them at a golf course. This invited trouble, as someone reported this to the police. The cops came to the Buffetts' home to talk to the parents. Luckily for him, his parents remained calm about the mistake that he had made and did not ban Warren from doing other little businesses. The parents perhaps understood that their son had a flair for earning money, and he was just a child when this incident happened. At around 10 years of age, Warren was selling popcorn and peanuts at university football games. His collection of coins was growing.

Early Exposure to the Stock Market

Warren often visited his father's stockbrokerage office. The environment there, expectedly, was infused with the talk of investment, profit and loss. Always finding an opportunity to read, Warren started reading the books in his father's office. He got particularly fond of reading 'The Trader' column in the financial newspaper *Barron's*, published by Dow Jones and Company. Incidentally, another stock-broking company was located in the same building as Howard Buffett's office. Warren would often stroll into this office. Here, he not only listened to animated conversations about the stock market, but also got the first hands-on exposure to stock prices. He got the opportunity to write stock prices on a chalkboard, something that he thought was a stylish thing to do. During this time, it was discovered that Warren had some difficulty in reading fine print. He was found to be having some trouble with his vision, and was prescribed glasses, something that define his appearance till date.

Spectacles did not cause any hindrances in the child's interest in reading and working with numbers. Curiously, 10-year-old Warren did not get bored in the company of adults discussing numbers and money. On the contrary, he felt happy about it. As he started enjoying the company of grown-up people more, he started forming his own ideas about the importance of having money.

The First Trip to the NYSE

Warren's 10th birthday brought with it a memorable event that proved to be a significant factor in shaping his life. Warren's father had committed himself to gifting a trip to each of his three children when they turned 10. When Warren was asked where he wanted to go, he mentioned three places in New York, among which, one was the New York Stock Exchange (NYSE). While a 10-year-old's interest in a stock exchange was unusual in itself, this child's observation and readings of that place was no less remarkable.

The stock market at that time was recovering from the Depression, and even with the crowd of busy people, the atmosphere was ordinary. As Warren went around with his father, he could see that even in difficult times, there were some people who seemed to be able to afford luxury. He could make out that somehow this place helped people earn a lot of money. That left a lasting impression on his mind. The importance of earning money became even clearer to him.

A little while before he stepped into the NYSE, Warren had had another experience that he wouldn't ever forget. His father had dropped in to meet Sidney Weinberg, the famous partner of Goldman Sachs, one of the most well-known investment firms. As the two adults conversed, the child looked around the office and he knew he was in the company of someone incredibly important. At the end of the meeting, Weinberg playfully asked the little child, 'What stock do you like, Warren?'[1]

This must have been a casual remark for Weinberg, but for Warren, it was momentous, something that he would remember for life. He took the remark as Weinberg's interest in his opinion. Interestingly, years later, Warren Buffett would become one of the biggest shareholders of Goldman Sachs.

The trip to New York affected Warren profoundly. It intensified the already existing desire in his mind to earn money. He could figure out that somehow the stock exchange was a road to becoming rich. More importantly, he felt money could make a person independent. He was fascinated with the idea of doing things the way he wanted to if he had good money. He had seen enough in the after-effects of the Depression to figure out that having financial constraints was not a good thing for anyone.

Ideas Find a Direction

As if Warren's questions were waiting to be answered, he chanced upon a book titled *One Thousand Ways to Make $1000* by the American author Frances Cowan Minaker. The book has long been out of print, but it is still famous as the book that inspired Buffett to start his first real business. As soon as he saw that book in a library, he was fascinated with it and read through it eagerly. The book was meant to inspire readers to invest as early as they could. It explained how the time was right to make many kinds of investments and used inspirational language to motivate people to think about taking a plunge into a business.

The book also suggested various ways by which a person could make a minuscule investment of a few dollars, and turn it into a thousand dollars. That was perfect for Warren, who had not only been saving his money but also wanted to grow it. He began to understand the benefits of compounding, how a small amount of money could grow into greater amounts. The concept of compounding would be something that would become vital for him in the years to come. One of the business ideas mentioned in the book was that of weighing scales. The idea was that if pennyweight scales were bought and installed in certain public places like shops, people would drop a coin to weigh themselves. The owner of the place would share the profit, but even then, one could earn money without putting in any effort. The money earned could be used to buy more machines, and, hence, the profit would keep increasing.

Most people are familiar with the famous anecdote that at the age of 11, Warren had announced that he was going to be a millionaire by the age of 35. But where did this confidence come from? As he read this book, Warren got fascinated with the magic of compounding. He sat down to calculate and worked out that the sooner he started, the better would be his chances of growing money earlier than most people. This was not innocent talk; he had worked out the numbers. By the age of 12, he had saved $120 doing small jobs.

The First Investment

The time had come for Warren to try his hand at the concepts he had been gradually following. He was aware that his father had often recommended stocks of Cities Service Preferred to his clients. He convinced his sister Doris to invest with him, and for both of them, he bought six shares of the company for $38.25 a share. Though Warren was barely 12 at this time, he learnt important lessons in investing through this event.

Within weeks of buying these shares, their prices dropped to $27 a share. Warren's disappointment increased when his sister constantly bugged him about the loss they had run into. As soon as the stock recovered and the price came to $40, a concerned Warren sold the shares and shared the minor profit with his sister. A burden had been let off him, but he learnt a lesson for life, when soon the price of each share rose to $202. He saw the importance of being patient. Had he waited a while, he would have made a substantial profit. Another lesson that meant a lot for him was being careful when investing someone else's money. He never forgot how his sister felt at the initial loss. Even as he grew up, he avoided being the reason for other people's disappointment.

A Great Change

In 1942, Warren Buffett's life took a different turn. His father ran for the US House of Representatives and got elected. Along with his family, Warren had been campaigning for his father but wasn't aware of the change that could ensue. When Howard was elected, the family had to move to Washington, D.C. The change in place meant losing friends and many things that made him comfortable. He missed the old environment terribly and his performance at school suffered. When his parents saw that he appeared to be in distress, they sent him to live with his grandfather, Ernest, for a few months.

Back at Omaha, Warren went back to his old school, Rosehill. Ever so interested in making money, on the weekends, Warren went to work at his grandfather's grocery store, where he did odd jobs. He also collected newspapers and magazines from the neighbourhood, and sold them with help from Aunt Alice. In addition, Warren read through all the issues of the *Progressive Grocer* magazine that his grandfather had, giving him an additional insight into how this business worked.

Warren was happy at his grandfather's house, except that he was made to eat fruits and vegetables, something that he never really cherished. He would avoid broccoli and asparagus as far as possible, a habit that he has continued with.

Soon, he discovered his sister Doris's bicycle that the family had left behind when they had moved to Washington. Warren started using this bike and enjoyed the experience. What went wrong was that without his sister's consent, he sold it off to buy a boy's bicycle with the money. Though Doris got angry when she discovered this, the elders let go of him easily. He thus had a bike of his 'own' now, though the means with which he had acquired it were unfair.

The Buffett family came to Omaha for the summer and Howard bought the South Omaha Feed Company in order to get some additional income. Warren worked at his father's company for a while but did not like manual labour.

Back in Washington with his family, he started attending Alice Deal Junior High School. He gradually adjusted to the new school and new friends, but his academic performance was not good. All the same, his continuous endeavours of doing small jobs continued and he became a newspaper delivery boy. He used his bicycle to deliver *The Washington Post, The Times Herald* and *The Evening Star.* Warren rather enjoyed this whole exercise. His fascination with newspapers was growing, and it translated into his desire to own publishing houses much later in life.

On the Wrong Path

The disappointment Warren had been feeling on leaving Omaha led him to think of a dangerous plan. He decided to run away from home. He had started playing golf with a couple of his friends and had also briefly worked as a caddie. That gave him the confidence that he and the boys could sustain themselves by caddying at a golf course. He convinced his two friends to run away from home with him to Pennsylvania, where they could work at a popular golf course. The boys travelled around 150 miles till the police got suspicious and detained them. They insisted that they were travelling with their parents' permission and, after a great deal of questioning, were let off. Warren was scared and also felt guilty of having put his own parents and the parents of his friends in a difficult situation.

Sometime after this incident, Warren got involved in

another questionable activity — he started stealing from a store. Along with his friends, he would smuggle out golf balls and other things from a store called Sears. He lied to his parents about this stuff lying in his room. He never got caught, but he was moving fast on a criminal path. Along with this, his performance in school was going downhill. The teachers portrayed a bleak future for him, but his parents somehow continued supporting him. Secretly, they were concerned. Warren's father gave him two straight options, either to behave appropriately or to give up his newspaper-vending jobs. The latter was too important for Warren; hence he started making every effort to stay away from dubious activities.

Warren Buffett Becomes a Taxpayer

By 1944, Warren Buffett had saved $1,000. At the age of 14, he filed his first income tax return. Thinking like a savvy businessman, he got a rebate for his 'expenses' too. He listed his bicycle and wristwatch as business expenses and got a deduction for these. The watch and the bike definitely played an important role in Warren's job routine. He was particular about delivering the newspapers on time and enjoyed getting up early and going for the deliveries. He had even taken up a delivery route in the afternoons. His pile of savings was increasing and teenaged Warren was inching closer to his goal of becoming a millionaire.

YOUTH AND HIGHER EDUCATION

By the time Buffett was in 10th grade, he had already gained a reputation as a student who was also a businessman. This was an extremely rare distinction, and at Woodrow Wilson High School, the school that Buffett attended in Washington, there was probably no other kid who was doing the same. In addition, Buffett had a bounty of $2,000, which he had earned by his own efforts—his savings from his childhood ventures. That was not a small amount for those times. Buffett's constant quest to explore ways of earning more and more money distinguished him from the other students. He never looked back and continued with various ventures.

He was around 15 years of age when he got his father's permission to invest in a hardware store called Builders Supply Corporation. He still worked as a newspaper vendor, and surprisingly, earned a substantial amount of money through it, more than some of his teachers. More interesting were a number of small businesses that he started. He sourced used but refurbished golf balls from a dealer and sold these to individuals. He also started a car-buffing business from a garage at one of his friends' houses, taking him as a partner. However, he soon gave this up as it required working laboriously. In addition, he sold collectable stamps.

While these businesses more or less suited a school kid, Buffett had already started doing the big stuff as well. He spent $1,200 to buy a 40-acre farm in Nebraska. He had zero interest in becoming a farmer; this was another kind of investment for him as he lent the farm to a tenant who worked on it. The two shared the profit.

As a student, Buffett was different from the others as far as 'normal' socializing went. He felt more comfortable with elders than with people his own age. People took him to be a serious guy and that hurt his efforts at fitting into peer groups. Sometime earlier, he had read Dale Carnegie's bestselling book *How to Win Friends and Influence People*. He re-studied the rules mentioned in the book and applied them to his interactions with other people, and gradually attained reasonably satisfying results. Now, he had started gathering social skills to complement the business skills that he inherently had.

The Pinball Machine Business

The book *One Thousand Ways to Make $1000* had given Buffett many ideas, but at 17 years of age, when he got a chance to buy an old pinball machine, he saw a real opportunity to put the ideas from that book into practice. He brought in his friend Don Danley as a partner. The latter repaired and smartened up the machine. The duo convinced a local barber to install the machine in his shop. That was a novel idea and many customers who came to the shop didn't mind spending a few coins to have fun at the machine. In just a week, the machine had given back enough profit for Buffett to recover his $25 even after sharing half of it with the shop owner. Buffett was excited. He bought another pinball machine with this capital and very soon, he had installed around eight such machines in other barber shops. At 17, he had earned $5,000, and more importantly, he had experienced how money could grow itself.

Starting College

When Buffett graduated from high school, his skill with investing money had become well-known. His photo in the school yearbook had the caption: 'Future stock broker'. That prediction did come true sometime later, but at the age of 17, his parents wanted him to pursue a business degree from the University of Pennsylvania. Buffett however had other plans. He thought he knew how to make sufficient amounts of money and did not want to waste time pursuing higher education. His father persisted, and to honour his wish, Warren enrolled at the Wharton School of Business at Pennsylvania.

At Pennsylvania, Buffett found himself different from the crowd. Intellectually, he was tough competition. He surprised people with his great power of memorizing, and his keen interest in the stock market impressed quite a few. Even in discussions on politics, he was impressive, given his first-hand experience of his father being a member of the US Congress. He even joined the youth wing of the Republican party at the college.

However, when it came to socializing, he found himself in awkward situations, especially where girls were concerned. He did join the Alpha Sigma Phi fraternity, the secret brotherhood that his father had joined in his college days, but that didn't contribute much to his efforts of fitting in. He was different.

Buffett wasn't really enjoying this life at college, and respite came to him in disguise. When he had been at Wharton for around two years, the family had to move back to Nebraska. His father had lost the election this time, as he was always more of an idealist than a practical politician. While his father's defeat made him sad, the opportunity to go back to the place he loved excited him. He transferred to the University of Nebraska, and once he was back, true to his nature, he quickly found ways of earning more money. He first became a manager for a team of newspaper-delivery people. Then he found a job at the famous store JCPenney. He also restarted his golf ball business, taking the help of one of his friends from Washington.

The Turning Point: Rejection by Harvard

By the time Buffett graduated in Business Administration from the University of Nebraska, he had been collecting not just cash through his business ventures but also a treasure of valuable experiences. However, his eyes were firmly fixed on his childhood goal of becoming a millionaire by the age of 35. Closely connected to this goal were his plans of applying to Harvard Business School after graduation. He felt that an education at that institution would open many doors for him. He had even secured a scholarship to sponsor his education, though he also had the money provided by his father for his education. Buffett appeared for the admission interview with full confidence but the interviewer thought differently. Buffett was rejected and was told that he would perhaps be eligible sometime in the future.

Buffett was naturally upset, more so because he thought his father would be disappointed. However, Howard was an understanding father and as always, he never put pressure on Warren to meet certain targets. Probably, Howard had a vague idea of his son's potential.

The Harvard rejection proved to be a turning point in Warren Buffett's life. In his own words, 'It turned out to be the best thing that ever happened to me.'[2] The rejection made Buffett look for other options, and led him to Benjamin Graham, an investor he idolized. Buffett had been reading many books about investing, but Graham's book *The Intelligent Investor* had interested him the most. He had also been captivated by *Security Analysis*, a book that Benjamin Graham had co-authored with David L. Dodd. While looking for colleges, Buffett came across the information that both Graham and Dodd taught at the Department of Finance at Columbia University. He couldn't believe it. A dream opportunity was staring him in his face.

There was one problem, though. It was too late to apply to the university; the semester was about to begin in a few days. Buffett was not the one to give up his dream so easily. He tried an unconventional way and wrote a letter to Dodd, Head of the Department of Finance at Columbia. The letter was candid to say the least. It read, 'I thought you guys were dead, but now that I've found out that you're alive, and teaching at Columbia, I would really like to come.'[3] Warren Buffett was taken in, bypassing the formalities of the deadline.

At Columbia with Ben Graham

Buffett has pointed out numerous times that having Dodd and Graham as his teachers was the turning point in his life. At Columbia Business School, he was learning from people whom he had come to idolize. But more importantly, the two teachers specialized in the art of investing—a skill that was meant to be Buffett's destiny. The setting turned out to be perfect for him, as now, he could sharpen his understanding of the subject that interested him the most. Buffett was the most responsive and attentive student in the class, and as always, he was impressive with his memory. It is said that he could recall exact figures and examples from *Security Analysis*, something that even Dodd could not do.

The most important aspects of this phase in his life, however, were the things he learnt from Graham. Buffett idolized Graham, and his reason for joining this university was to learn directly from him. But other than investing, he didn't really share Graham's interest in classic literature and the arts. Neither did he have any idea of the morally questionable alliances that Graham had with many women. He was obsessed with learning

Graham's approach towards value investing.

Buffett learnt some crucial things from Graham, which have formed the basis of his investment strategy all through his life. Graham was always extremely wary of investments that involved risks, and presumably, the most important lesson that Buffett got from Graham was always having a 'margin of safety'. Graham had called these three words the most important in investing. Buffett followed through on this principle, which basically means that an investor would be in a comfortable position if he understands that price and value of a share are not the same thing, and an investor can minimize his potential loss by understanding this. In Graham's words, 'Buy stocks the way you buy groceries, not perfume.'[4]

Graham's method of teaching too impressed Buffett. Graham had devised the concept of 'Mr Market', an allegorical character from his book *The Intelligent Investor*. Mr Market has great mood swings, from extreme pessimism to over optimism, and he entices investors to behave according to his highly emotional reactions. Through this character, Graham effectively drove home the point that investing should not be based on such fluctuations but rather on solid analysis.

Yet, Mr Market can help careful investors buy and sell at appropriate times, since he has extreme reactions to market fluctuations. Buffett did apply this principle a number of times in his career. As Buffett kept on absorbing information from his favourite teacher, in the classroom, it was amply clear that he was the most brilliant student. His classmates noticed his incredible capacity to not only focus on a topic but to maintain the focus throughout, without getting tired or distracted.

It is remarkable that while Buffett almost worshipped Graham, he did not blindly follow the latter's principles. He disagreed with his teacher's ideas many times and thought for himself when it came to putting the ideas to practice. The most prominent example of this is the stock of Government Employees Insurance Company, GEICO. Graham did not approve of these shares, but Buffett used about 75 per cent of his net worth to buy this stock in GEICO. This he did after intensively researching the company, even travelling to Washington to visit the company office. He was fascinated with the business idea and was sure it would turn out good. Though Buffett worked like an independent thinker, Graham's stamp on him was not something that could be worn out easily.

BACK IN OMAHA

Another Rejection

After completing his formal education, it was time for Buffett to begin a conventional career. This situation was a bit strange, given that he had been building his career since his childhood, and was in many ways, already a serious businessman. Yet, he felt that he could learn more if he worked for Ben Graham. While at Columbia, Buffett had been getting increasingly convinced that he should work for the Graham-Newman Corporation, a small firm that Graham ran with Jerry Newman, his business partner. None of the students dared to ask the great Benjamin Graham to hire them, but for a long time, Buffett had nurtured a deep desire to work for Graham. He took the formidable step. He was confident that he had the skills. In addition, he had been an outstanding student in his class. To increase his chances, he planned that he would offer to work for free.

Graham turned down Buffett's proposal of working for him. He gave a reason that was coloured with the peculiar socio-political situation of those times. Jews were having a hard time finding employment anywhere in America, including Wall Street. Graham had made it a policy to hire only Jews, so he wouldn't change it even for one of his most favourite students. Dejected, Buffett came back to Omaha. Secretly though, he did not give up. He was hopeful that sometime in the future, he might be able to work for Graham.

In Omaha as a Stockbroker

This rejection brought Buffett back to Omaha. He hadn't really planned to do anything other than work for Graham, and hence, back in his hometown, he decided to become a stockbroker. His decision surprised many people, as the general perception was that to have a successful stockbroking business, one should be based in Wall Street. Buffett thought differently. He had been able to swell his capital to a little less than $20,000 at the age of 21, and he was confident about how he wanted to go ahead. As always, after a studious inspection of the stocks, he went ahead to invest even when others cautioned him not to. Buffett had always avoided borrowing money, but now, for the first time, he took a bank loan of $5,000 to expand his investing potential. This was a calculated move, as he saw great potential in the market that had been reviving itself for a long time after the depression.

Soon, Buffett joined his father's firm, Buffett-Falk & Co. He worked on commission basis at this company, selling shares to mostly friends and relatives. He was young and looked inexperienced, and it took people a while to take his advice seriously. Though he enjoyed the process of investing in stocks, he didn't feel comfortable acting as a salesman for the same. He kept following through with Graham.

Fear of Public Speaking

Meanwhile, Buffett was getting increasingly conscious of a personal drawback. He was 'terrified' of public speaking. All through his school and college, he had been feeling the necessity of overcoming this fear, especially when interacting with girls. His stage fright was of an extreme kind; he would feel nauseated and even vomit before going for any kind of public speaking. Now, at Omaha, when he was working as a securities broker, he felt that to improve his prospects of getting more business, he would have to talk to people, and for that, he would have to get rid of his fear. He had liked the ideas mentioned in Carnegie's book *How to Win Friends and Influence People*. As chance would have it, he happened to see an advertisement for a Carnegie public-speaking course in New York.

Buffett went up, taking with him the fee of $100 in the form of a cheque. However, he lost the nerve soon, and stopped payment for the cheque. Avoiding the course seemed to do him no good, so sometime later, he gathered up sufficient courage to join the course. This time, he took cash with him, and deposited the fee before he would be tempted to change his mind.

The public-speaking course gave Buffett a new life. The extent to which this course changed his life can be judged from the fact that he proudly declares the Dale Carnegie course to be the most important degree of his life. The displays in his office do not include his degrees from the University of Nebraska or from

Columbia University, but the Dale Carnegie certificate, which enjoys a prominent place among the displays. This skill of public speaking that he learnt at Carnegie proved to be an important tool in his success. He told an interviewer, 'That $100 course gave me the most important degree I have. It's certainly had the biggest impact in terms of my subsequent success.' He added, 'In graduate school, you learn all this complicated stuff, but what's really essential is being able to get others to follow your ideas.'[5]

Buffett was careful enough not to forget the lessons of the course. In order to stay in the practice of communicating, he started taking night classes at the University of Omaha. He thoroughly enjoyed the role of a teacher, especially when it was on his favourite topic – investing.

Setbacks

As Buffett continued with life at Omaha, he got increasingly interested in reading through *Moody's Manuals*, which were sometimes as voluminous as 10,000 pages. He had been in a habit of reading these manuals, patiently going through details of different companies in the country. He also continued studying Graham and Dodd's book. As he was continuously learning, he got new ideas. In this process, he made two decisions that proved to be financial mistakes, but enriched him with valuable lessons nevertheless.

The first of these was buying a textile company called Cleveland Textile Mills. He had encouraged a few other people too to buy the company's shares. The company paid a high dividend to the investors. Its share price was less than half the net current asset value. However, after the purchase, the company cut down the dividend, as it was facing tough competition from other mills. Buffett was extremely disappointed, especially since he had made other people invest in the shares. This episode, however, taught him the importance of strategic, competitive positioning of businesses.

The idea of acting as a stock-salesman wasn't really a very interesting prospect to Buffett, so he tried to own another business. With a friend as a partner, he bought a petrol station in Omaha. The location of the gas station turned out to be its biggest drawback, as it was located opposite a popular, established petrol station. Buffett did a lot of hard work, even doing manual labour, to make the business click. However, he could not make it profitable, as the other station had meticulously built a customer base and almost all the customers went there. Buffett lost $2,000 in the business, but learnt the importance of building a base of loyal customers.

At this stage, Buffett was left with no other option but to keep working as a stockbroker at his father's company, a job that he did not really like. He wanted to avoid the possibility of disappointing people with his stock suggestions. In his mind, he was always thinking of ways to expand his horizons. He got an offer to work as a money manager in New York, but due to his obligatory attendance at the National Guard, he was not permitted to leave the city.

In Love

While at the professional front, Buffett was not feeling satisfied, on the personal front, a beautiful story had stared unfolding in his life. During one of his home visits, when Buffett was still a student at Columbia, his sister Roberta had introduced him to a roommate of hers. She was Susan Thompson, daughter of a dean at the University of Omaha. Susan was a lively girl with an interest in art rather than academics. She was a social creature, liberal in her views. That set her apart from the others. People in those times were affected with racist prejudices, but not Susan. Ever since Buffett had met Susan, he had been attracted to her in many ways. He had dated another girl for a while, but for him, Susan was the one.

At Omaha, he tried to meet Susan and her family as many times as possible. Her father was a Republican supporter too, and had in fact managed an election campaign for Howard Buffett. He liked Buffett. Susan, however, was dating someone else and wasn't really interested in Buffett. It took some time for her to develop a liking for him. Once they started dating, Buffett was deeply in love and Susan gradually began to see the inherent goodness in this man. At the time when Buffett was doing well at his Dale Carnegie course, he encashed his confidence to propose to her. The two got engaged and were officially a couple. The interesting part was that though Buffett constantly thought of growing his money, Susan had no interest in the stock market or in the business of making money. A letter he wrote to one of his aunts gives an interesting insight into how he was balancing the two loves of his life. He wrote,

'This girl has only one drawback; she knows nothing about stocks. Otherwise, she is unbeatable and I guess I can overlook her Achilles' heel.'[6]

Filling the Emotional Gaps

Warren Buffett and Susan Thompson got married on 19 April 1952. The couple went for a long road trip for their honeymoon, visiting different places. It is said that Buffett had stacked ledgers and *Moody's Manuals* on the rear seat of the car. His interest in money was an inseparable part of his being, but Buffett was the happiest man because he thought he could not have got a better life partner. At the same time, he never lost sight of his other love – investing and making money. A particular incident during their honeymoon made him even more confident about his ability to make money. While at a casino in Las Vegas, he was surprised to see people continue to gamble and to lose money even when the odds of winning were negligible. He seemed to have noticed something about people's relationship with money at that time, and he declared to his wife that they would definitely make a lot of money.

Susan had no interest in growing money; her main concern was to fill in the gaps in her husband's life. She had recognized that Buffett needed care and support to overcome his emotional insecurities and to become a whole person. Her role in shaping the future Warren Buffett is unmistakably a big one. When she entered Buffett's life, he felt complete, and even more confident of achieving his career goals. It is no wonder that he credits Susan for making him complete and helping him become successful.

WORKING FOR HIS HERO

Changes in the Personal Landscape

As Buffett settled into married life with a caring and sensitive Susan, he experienced love and security in his personal life like never before. Childhood inhibitions that had been a result of his mother's peculiar condition started to fade away. That Susan had an unmistakably positive impact on him is clear from his words, 'I was a lopsided person. She put me together.'[7] The couple welcomed their first child, named after her mother, Susan Alice, on 30 July 1953. Parenthood added a soft responsibility to Buffett's busy days and nights, most of which were otherwise spent studying stocks and companies and in preparing reports.

Around the same time, Warren Buffett and his father launched their company Buffett & Buffett, to which the former contributed just a small amount of money, although he put in a lot in terms of work and ideas. At this time, Howard Buffett's political career had been declining. He was uncompromising in his principles, and some thought that he stretched his idealism too far. Consequently, he wound up his political life and moved back to the stockbrokerage business at Omaha. The father–son duo built their partnership Buffett & Buffett and continued with the stockbrokerage work they had been doing. Even in the low phase of his father's political career, Warren could clearly see the lessons. He loved his father and had immense respect for him, but at the same time, he could see that rigid idealism could leave a person alone. He must have sensed a need to strike a balance between principles and the need to have associates. Warren Buffett is greatly respected for his ethics as well as for his humility with people — traits that might have their roots in his observations of his father's experience.

Dream Comes True

Buffett had never lost sight of his goal of becoming a millionaire. But there was another wish that he had kept close to his heart—that of working for Ben Graham. Though it had been two years since he had been denied the opportunity to work for the legend, he had been meticulously keeping in touch with him. He even went up to meet Graham occasionally. His profound wish came true when he was called over by Graham-Newman, telling him they had changed their mind and wanted to hire him. Nothing could make Buffett happier at that time. The family moved to New York, and famously, he showed up at the office a month before his date of joining. It was a company of just seven employees and Buffett proudly became the eighth one.

Buffett had acquired his public speaking skills after a great deal of struggle; hence he was careful enough not to let them fade away. While he immersed himself at work in Graham-Newman, he also took classes at an adult school, teaching investing to people. By the end of the year, on 15 December 1954, Susan and Buffett were blessed with their second child, Howard Graham. Now a father of two, Buffett's family responsibilities increased, but his wife took care of most of the domestic affairs and he worked day and night on his investing ideas. His famous habit of thriftiness was now well-known to his wife, and the family lived in a rented apartment rather than buying a house.

Useful 'Cigar Butts'

Working for Graham-Newman was a vital phase of learning in Buffett's journey. Here, too, he continued with his habit of meticulously studying the manuals that listed public companies. This was a tedious task as these manuals run into thousands of pages and were full of numbers and figures, but Buffett thoroughly enjoyed it; he had of course been enjoying numbers since his childhood. This skill became an asset for the company and, soon, both Graham and Newman came to value Buffett as an important associate. He was assigned some important deals that turned out well. Buffett's skills and his capacity for hard work were recognized by the man he revered. What was more important for him, though, was what he sought to learn from Graham.

Of the things that Buffett learnt from Graham, the 'cigar butt' investing is perhaps the most prominent. Graham had a theory about locating companies which, just like the discarded cigar butts, had one last puff left in them. These were undervalued stocks that could be bought cheaply. Even if they looked bad, one last puff could be extracted from them. For Graham, making such small investments also maintained a margin of safety. Buffett followed this method of investing for a long time, but at the same time, he maintained his independent thought process. Unlike Graham, he did not diversify much. After careful study of the listed companies, he narrowed down to the ones that would be the best investments. Graham, on the other hand, was obsessed with diversification. That helped him stay within safe margins.

Buffett studied every company that he could find information on and these were sometimes very small ones and were not traded on the stock exchange. Many times, he even visited the companies to see the management and the actual business. After a careful study, he bought cheap stocks and earned a great margin of profit on those. Buffett could see opportunities everywhere and on a personal level, to raise more capital to invest for himself, he sold off his cherished GEICO shares. His efforts paid off, and he was gradually increasing his pile of money.

Buffett's performance at Graham-Newman was brilliant, but one impressive feat at this time stands out. While researching various public companies, he discovered the Union Street Railway, which was offering stocks at cheap rates. Buffett sensed an opportunity and bought into it. He made a profit of $20,000 in a few weeks' time. It was an extraordinary amount in the year 1955. The same cigar butt methodology had worked wonders once again.

Buffett was enjoying his time at Graham-Newman, but he soon sensed the probability that this might not last too long. Within a year, Graham and Newman were planning to retire. This soon turned into reality, when Graham announced his retirement in mid-1956. The situation brought a mixture of sadness and joy for Buffett. He did not want to stay in the company when Graham was not around, but he felt immensely privileged when Graham wanted him to take over as one of the partners of the firm. This was the most rewarding thing for Buffett, as Graham-Newman Corporation was famous, and Graham trusted his former student to the extent of passing on the company to him.

It was certainly not an easy decision for Buffett. He had gotten the chance of a lifetime to replace his mentor in the company. Buffett had reverential regard for Graham. Yet, he did not want to stay on if he did not get to work with him. For many days, Buffett gathered up the courage to communicate his denial. He finally declined the offer.

If he was not going to work with Graham, there was no charm staying back in New York, so he decided to move back to Omaha. This was not entirely an emotional decision though. Buffett was convinced about what he wanted. His decision to continue with his investment business in Omaha was unconventional to say the least, but he was confident about his ability to pull it off, even when he worked away from the buzz of the great New York City. It remained to be seen how his unusual choice would shape his future.

THE PARTNERSHIPS

Retiring at 26

When Buffett shifted back to Omaha after his stint at Graham-Newman, he carried with him a wealth of knowledge and experience. Interestingly, he also carried back with him the more obvious wealth. He had grown richer quickly, with a net worth of around $174,000. The cigar butt investing, powered by his smart selection of stocks had profited him, as had his annual salary of $12,000, which in those times, was more than thrice the amount of an average person's income. His savings were growing at a rate that would help him get closer to his goal of becoming a millionaire by 35.

Back in Omaha, he settled down with his wife and two kids in a rented house, and mentioned the peculiar idea of 'retiring'. He was just 26 years of age and was passionate about increasing his pile of money. This idea thus sounded cryptic, if not weird. What Buffett really meant by 'retiring' was that he would like to use a small part of his savings to give a comfortable life to his family and the major chunk of it would go into further investments. He wanted to turn his money into capital for smarter investments.

Noticeably, Buffett was never comfortable working for anyone; Graham had been an exception. Neither did he want to get into professional relationships that would put an emotional burden of causing a loss to anyone he worked with. He also did not like to be judged by other people on the way he was investing. In short, he did not want a boss or a professional partner to work with. At the same time, he felt that the partnership idea like Graham-Newman was a good one. Therefore, he came up with the idea of setting a partnership with people he would be comfortable with. He also loved the idea of working as a fiduciary money manager, helping people grow their savings.

Buffett Associates, Ltd

Buffett was clear that he did not want to get into a partnership with people who would be critical of his way of working. In addition, he did not want to invest all of his capital into a partnership. At the same time, a few of his friends and relatives suggested to him that he manage their money. That was a perfect setting. He wouldn't have to work for a boss and could still do what he liked. Thus, he invited six people who trusted him to form a partnership. These were the people who wouldn't criticize or judge him for his choices. This group included his aunt Alice, who contributed the largest sum of $35,000. Buffett's father-in-law, Dr William Thompson, was always supportive of him, and he pitched in with a contribution of $25,000. His roommate from Wharton Business School, Chuck Peterson contributed $5,000, while his mother, Elizabeth, put in $25,000. Dan Monen, Buffett's childhood friend, had now become his lawyer and he put in $5,000. Buffett's sister Doris and her husband put in $10,000. Buffett himself, the seventh partner in the firm, invested $100 only. Thus, he had made a smart move — he had raised the capital to start the partnership, and at the same time, he had the major part of his personal funds available as capital for separate ventures. It was an important requirement for him to have his personal funds available for investing elsewhere. This was because he did not want to withdraw any money from the partnership, but he needed around $12,000 every year to finance his family's needs. He would use the surplus, in his characteristic style, as capital to compound his money even faster.

It is noteworthy that inviting family and friends to put their money into the partnership, demonstrates the level of confidence that Buffett had in his own abilities. He greatly valued these relationships and could not imagine bringing a loss to any of these people. In fact, at this stage, he did not imagine he would ever lose money. Growth of wealth was the only future he believed in.

To lay down the terms of the partnership, he arranged a dinner meeting of the partners, where the bill was shared by all the attendees. By this time, people had started getting used to Buffett's famous habit of thriftiness. In the meeting, he communicated the way the partnership would work, as always, taking precaution that nobody should be disappointed because of his investing decisions. He was the general partner of the firm while the others were limited partners. The rules were simple — the limited partners would receive a 4 per cent interest for their investment. For a profit above 4 per cent, Buffett would get a 50 per cent of profits, but in case of losses, he would cover 25 per cent of the losses. Further, he imposed upon himself an unlimited obligation to cover the losses.

Soon after the founding of Buffett Associates, he wound up his matters at New York. The fact that an educated, young man with a good understanding of the stock market wouldn't work at NYSE seemed outlandish to the people of those times. New York was the place where any stock business could be done, according to the general feeling of those days. Buffett, however, thought differently. As far as investing smartly was concerned, he was confidence personified. Besides, he thought that the hyperactive environment of New York would only act as a distraction. He did not think he needed constant influencing from other people in the stock market. A better definition of self-belief is hard to find.

When Buffett had closed his affairs in New York, he drove down for a few days on his way to Omaha, visiting various companies on the way. His wife and kids had already gone back. Buffett was always on the lookout for interesting businesses and hence interesting investment ideas. When he reached Omaha, he entered a fresh phase of his life. At the same time, he kept on polishing his public speaking skills, this time taking up three classes at the University of Omaha. He was constantly aware of the need to communicate effectively if he was to convince people about his ideas.

Buffett Fund, Ltd

Buffett had always loved the idea of working as a professional money manager for people. He had been doing this work as a fiduciary for a few friends and acquaintances. But a huge opportunity came to him in the form of a recommendation from none other than Ben Graham. A professor and president of Norwich University named Homer Dodge had been investing in Graham-Newman. As the firm closed and Dodge had little idea whom to entrust his money with, Graham suggested Buffett to him. Dodge met Buffett in Omaha and another partnership took shape. This was a bigger deal than Buffett Associates because the amount was

$120,000, thus, more than the first partnership, and now, Buffett was officially a money manager. This time, he was not just managing money for friends and relatives.

Success and More Partnerships

John Cleary, a person who had worked with Howard Buffett, invested with Warren Buffett to form a third partnership, the **B-C Partnership**. They raised a capital of $55,000. By the end of the year 1956, as a money manager, Buffett was working with around half a million dollars' worth of partnerships. As the year ended, he had beaten the market by about 4 per cent, with a profit of $4,500.

Buffett had also entered into a separate partnership with his friend Monen. The duo invested in an insurance company called National American Fire Insurance. Buffett had discovered this unbelievably cheap stock while doing his favourite thing — reading through *Moody's Manuals*. Monen did some footwork for Buffett, and the two outsmarted a local competitor to acquire 10 per cent of the company's shares.

In the next two years, he formed seven partnerships, in addition to maintaining his original partnership with his father, Buffett & Buffett. In the middle of 1957, he formed **The Underwood Partnership** with Chuck Peterson's mother with a capital of $85,000. A little later that year, he formed the **Dacee Partnership** in which Buffett was to manage $100,000 for a family of five members. This family was Dr Edwin Davis, his wife Dorothy and their three children. By this time, Monen had made a generous amount of profit from the National American Insurance shares. In 1958, Monen wanted to invest $70,000 on behalf of himself and his wife. Thus, came across Buffett's next partnership called the **Mo-Buff Partnership**. The seventh partnership had formed by February 1959. This was The **Glenoff Partnership**, formed with two sons of the prominent Offutt family of Omaha, and William Glenn, a businessman from the same city.

Having more partnerships fetched Buffett more fees and also more shares in the profits. He was raising increasing amounts of money for further investments, something that gave him great satisfaction, and also brought him closer to his goal. All along, he continued to use his personal funds to invest in cheap stocks and his personal wealth was growing too.

Unique Style of Working

Buffett was an unconventional investor, not just because he worked away from the hustle and bustle of the stock exchange, but also because when he explained his style of working to his partners, they were taken by surprise. When he started the partnerships, he made it clear that he would not declare where he was investing the partners' money, though he would send them a statement, once at the end of the year. He wouldn't discuss the investments so that he had complete control over investing decisions. The partners could decide to withdraw their money or to reinvest, but only at the end of the year. He did not like to be criticized and he did not want to disclose his course of action. The bottom line was, he was working mostly according to Graham's style of value investing.

A Trickster or a Genius?

Not surprisingly, Buffett's rules for his partners raised eyebrows. His refusal to disclose the course of action of the investments raised suspicion of him being a fraudulent investor who could be running a Ponzi scheme. Author Alice Schroeder in *The Snowball: Warren Buffett and the Business of Life* has even accounted that people got so suspicious that the Omaha Country Club had blacklisted him from taking a membership. Buffett managed to have the ban removed.

Despite the scepticism, his dexterity with money was gradually becoming more visible to people. His name had started doing the rounds in investment circles. A few prominent people of the town had invested with him. Buffett was doing what he had always wanted to do—compound money, or in other words, use money to grow more money.

Remarkable Profits

In the world of investing, the phrase 'beating the market' is often used but seldom achieved. But with a man like Warren Buffett, who had been dreaming of compounding money since his childhood, incredible things were bound to happen. It was not just the percentage of his fee that was increasing; his petty investment of a hundred dollars in each of the partnerships had grown into an unbelievable share of around 10 per cent ownership of the partnerships. The first year after forming the partnerships, he had earned more than 10 per cent, though the market had fallen 8 per cent. Due to his reinvestments, there was a 40 per cent increase in the value of the partnerships. Again in 1959, he outperformed the market by 6 per cent. A year later, the partnerships achieved an incredible feat—they beat the market by 29 per cent. Buffett was pacing towards his goal of becoming a millionaire.

The Atypical Rich Man

Buffett was not only making a name for himself in the investing world, but was also growing richer. However, in no way did his lifestyle demonstrate his wealth or the stature of his work. Though he could afford a house well before this, he bought his first house in 1958, and paid an amount of $31,500 for the modest five-bedroom house. Soon after moving into this house, Susan and Warren Buffett were blessed with their third child, Peter.

The fact that his wife spent about $15,000 to furnish and decorate the house was incomprehensible to Buffett. However, he came to terms with it quickly since he loved his wife and wanted her to be happy. Left to himself, he could only think of this amount as capital that could have given great returns. Though Buffett had jokingly nicknamed the house Buffett's Folly, years later, in an interview to the *Business Insider*, he called it the 'third best investment he had ever made.'[8] This is not surprising since Buffett has never bought another house to live in. He continues living in this house at Farnam Street in Omaha and its value of course has grown many times.

His shock at the amount that his wife had spent on the house was just one of the traits that came to define Warren Buffett. He always tried to minimize spending. This trait is perhaps not just because of his thriftiness, but also because of his dislike for extravagance. While managing all those partnerships, he worked from a small room at his house. He loved spending most of the time in his den, and worked alone for the most part, doing all the paperwork himself and depositing documents in the bank personally. He typed all the letters on a manual typewriter and also did not engage anyone to file his returns. He even used the phone at home for work instead of getting another telephone connection. A little later, as the requirements grew, he took the help of a few associates like Monen.

Buffett wasn't particularly known to dress up smartly.

He is often reported to have been wearing simple clothing, without any particular attention to size or fit. Even in his youth, he was busy figuring out numbers rather than bothering about projecting an appearance. With these peculiar traits, and extraordinarily brainwork, Buffett was fast moving towards not just reaching his goal but also surpassing it.

GROWTH AND BEYOND

The late 1950s saw Buffett picking up his pace towards his goal of becoming a millionaire. Buffett's journey was propelled by his unwavering determination to achieve what he wanted. There was nothing that could distract him, not even his little children, who demanded his attention, often with their pranks and tantrums. A loving father, Buffett cuddled his children, spent time with them, was there when needed, but simultaneously, kept his mind at work, thinking of stocks. Comforted by the presence of his supportive wife, he worked long hours. His office was still a small room at his house. His reputation among investors was growing, but he also faced scepticism from many people. He hardly cared about the detractors. What he cared for was the cigar butts lying around, waiting to be put to use, excellent use, if Buffett was handling them.

Enter Charlie Munger

During this time when Buffett was engrossed in his mission, he happened to meet a person who was to play an increasingly important role in his life very soon. This man, whose appearance in the current time has become almost synonymous with Warren Buffett, was Charles Thomas Munger. Munger had served as a meteorologist in the US Army, was a Harvard Law School graduate and was working as a successful lawyer in California. He also loved making architectural designs. Originally from Omaha, Munger had even worked at Buffett's grandfather's grocery store during his school days, a fact that Buffett was unaware of till they met. So, years before their first meeting, the two had experienced the backbreaking work at Ernest's grocery store at different times and both had no fondness for manual labour.

In mid-1959, Munger was visiting Omaha, and a couple of his friends arranged a lunch meeting where their other friend Buffett was also present. Though Munger was working in a different occupation, his real interest was very similar to Buffett's; he was interested in making greater amounts of money. His passion for getting richer was not guided by a desire for a luxurious lifestyle, though. He liked the idea of becoming the master of his own life by reaching a certain monetary status. Like Buffett, it was a mission, and not greed, which drove him to study the art of multiplying money. Like Buffett, he was known as a humble person and believed in ethical ways of doing things. However, Munger's approach to investing was very different from Buffett's. There was a slim chance that these two men, six years apart in age and with strongly opposing points of view, would ever be friends.

However, both were mature, open-minded individuals. As soon as the two were introduced at the meeting, they could relate well with each other, yet at the same time, were genuinely interested in the other's contradictory points of view. The conversation got engrossing for both of them, and it is said that while the other two friends left after some time, Munger and Buffett were still in deep discussion. Munger had been thinking of starting his own investment business, and he got really interested in Buffett's storehouse of knowledge about the domain. For Buffett, Munger was one of the few individuals who understood investing, even though he was from an entirely different educational background and profession.

Munger went back to California taking with him a lifetime of friendship. It would be a few years later that Munger would join Buffett professionally, but the two men started having long discussions over the phone. Neither Buffett nor Munger was the one to waste time on social conversations; what they discussed was hardcore investing. Buffett's approach towards investing started taking a different flavour due to Munger's influence. As for Munger, he had recognized Buffett as a genius; he had identified the extraordinary qualities of this young man from Omaha. Munger put his observation into words when he told his wife, 'That is no ordinary human being.'[9]

Sanborn Map: A Meaningful Win

Buffett and Munger continued to have long-distance conversations. Meanwhile, Buffett was getting increasingly occupied as he took on larger projects. One of these was an undervalued stock of Sanborn Map, a company that created detailed maps to be used by insurance companies. Sensing a good opportunity, he invested one-third of the partnerships' money in this company and also bought the stock himself. The stock he purchased eventually got him to the board of the company. Soon, he figured out that the board was inefficient and shareholders wouldn't really have any advantage if things continued this way. Since he had got a considerable authority in the board, he took a strong stand and eventually had an agreement with the company in which the latter agreed to exchange shareholders' stock with a part of the investment portfolio. Buffett had not only earned a great profit for the shareholders, but had also managed to use his powers of convincing to push a deal. This time, he had not held on to the stock for a long time; the shift happened within two years.

Buffett Becomes a Millionaire

Buffett continued his keen study of the market and spotted opportunities smartly. He formed four more partnerships in addition to the previous seven, taking the number to 11. This included the **Emdee Partnership** with 11 doctors, **Ann Investments** for a known Omaha family, **Buffett-TD** for another business family and **Buffett-Holland** with two of his friends. By 1960, his reputation had grown exponentially among investors, though for the common people, he remained an ordinary man. He graduated from a person who had to convince people to invest with him, to a recognized investor who often received people from outside Omaha, requesting him to invest their money in his partnerships.

There was a minor hurdle, though. According to the law, there could not be more than a hundred partners. So, he asked people to club their money to keep the numbers in range. As would be the case with anyone moving towards success, there were a few naysayers around who predicted the doom of his empire. They were proved wrong. Compounding was doing wonders for Buffett and his partners. For him personally, the reinvested money made him an owner of 13 per cent of the partnerships' assets. Other than that, he had been working on his personal investments that were worth more than half a million dollars in 1960. With his combined assets, Buffett had become a millionaire by the age of 30, five years earlier than he had predicted as a child. This incredible feat cannot be ascribed to a couple of factors alone, but his tenacious determination was certainly the most outstanding reason.

Now a millionaire and a very busy investor, Buffett felt the need for a formal office space. Till then, he had not only been working from home, but was also doing most of the work single-handedly, even clerical work. Kiewit Plaza, Farnam Street became his office address from then on. Buffett had achieved a milestone, but that was definitely not the end of the toilsome road. That was just the achievement of a childhood dream. As it turned out, the journey had just begun.

HARD LESSONS AND A SHIFT IN STRATEGY

Millionaire Warren Buffett of Omaha was getting increasingly busy. In 1962, he decided to restructure his work by merging all of his partnerships into a single concern, which he named Buffett Partnership, Ltd (BPL). A couple of years ago, some people around the town had turned their noses up and predicted bankruptcy for this young man dealing in stocks. In those times, an educated man was supposed to be employed at a known company, and displaying the latest status symbols like cars and gadgets. With his air of mystery and distaste for flamboyance, Buffett did not really display the stereotypical image of a successful man. He, however, was amply clear about what he wanted.

His single-minded focus brought him to a stage where BPL began with $7.2 million as its net assets.

Unlike the earlier times, when Buffett had contributed just $100 to each of his partnerships, for the first time, he put in $450,000 into Buffett Partnership, Ltd (BPL). This happened to be a time when stocks had become cheaper because of the downward trends that the market was experiencing. There were quite a few cigar butts to be used, but this time, a choice that Buffett made had a great impact on him.

Dempster Mill Manufacturing

The Dempster episode in Buffett's life is a case that left mixed results of profit and caution for him. For around six years, beginning in 1956, Buffett had been investing partnership money into Dempster Mill Manufacturing, a company that made irrigation equipment and windmills. The stock was cheap, at $18 a share, while the book value was $72. The business had a peculiar social situation. It was located in Beatrice, a small town that heavily depended upon the company for employment. Buffett had started buying its stock at cheap rates, and continued doing so till he took control of the company as its chairman. However, he saw that profitability was low, and with the current management, there were lesser chances of improvement. He had invested 21 per cent of the partnership assets into Dempster, but the latter continued using up money. Since Buffett now regularly discussed his work with Munger, the latter recommended a turnaround specialist named Harry Bottle to manage the affairs. Bottle had expertise in turning around businesses and he soon rectified things at Dempster. The modifications included closing a few branches, raising the cost of spare parts, closing unprofitable lines, introducing changes in some business operations and liquidating a few assets. The profitability of the company increased and Dempster was pulled out of its sickness.

However, this had a dark personal side for Buffett. The alterations at Dempster had involved laying off more than a hundred people. Since there was no other major employer in town, this bought Buffett into the bad books of the townspeople. When Buffett tried to sell the company after the overhaul, it brought him further distrust. People were up in arms against Buffett bringing in another owner who might fire more people. The situation was resolved when the business was sold to First Beatrice Corporation. Financially, the matter ended well, getting about $42.3 million for Buffett's partnership, but in the future, Buffett wanted to be cautious against inviting any animosity towards himself.

Increasing Influence of Charlie Munger

Munger's presence in Buffett's life caused a sea change in the latter's philosophy of investing. Before this, Buffett staunchly believed in Graham's technique of looking for undervalued companies, the cigar butts. Most of Buffett's work had been centred around this concept. Munger had formed partnerships of his own to run similar investing businesses, and he too had been following the same technique for some time. But as the two men increasingly consulted each other, Munger convinced Buffett that they should start thinking differently. He had come to believe in buying good businesses at a good price, not the discarded cigar butts. One such opportunity came Buffett's way in 1963, in the form of a distressed American Express.

American Express: The Deal that Changed Buffett's Direction

As the year 1963 was drawing to its end, the very well-known American Express found itself deep in trouble due to a bad loan that it had issued. The company had been defrauded by Anthony 'Tino' De Angelis of a soybean oil company named Allied Crude Vegetable Oil. De Angelis had cheated banks by showing his oil assets as collateral to get huge loans. American Express was the guarantor in these transactions and was responsible for certifying the amount of oil the company had. Strangely, the amount of oil reported appeared to be more than the amount that could possibly be generated. Consequently, a great scam was discovered. De Angelis had filled the oil tanks with water, with just a film of soybean oil floating above it.

American Express's stock crashed, and more than that, people's trust in the company was at stake; the company was in the business of issuing credit cards and travellers' cheques worth millions to people around the world. If trust in the company was broken, all would be lost. Buffett did some ground research to find out about the popular perception of the company. The news was good. People still trusted the name. He started buying American Express shares. At this time, BPL had a capital of more than $17 billion to work with. By 1965, it had invested one-third of its money in American Express. Finally, the latter not only paid the settlement amount to the lenders but its share value too rose by more than $14 a share. This time, Buffett had worked with a giant in the market, not an undervalued company.

Berkshire Hathaway: The 'Dumbest' Thing that Buffett Did

The name 'Berkshire Hathaway', a formidable name in the contemporary context, is the international conglomerate founded by Buffett, with a net worth of over $570 billion as of February 2021. However, before the brand became what it is today, an interesting series of events ensued. The history goes back to the year 1962. Much as American Express made Buffett and his partners richer, there came along this episode that scarred Buffett's smooth ride towards more riches. This time, Buffett bought a sick business, lost money and knew it was a terrible decision.

However, it was not due to a misreading of the

stock; it was a vindictive reaction to what Buffett perceived as dishonesty. It seemed improbable that Buffett could take an emotional decision where stock was concerned, but it is important to understand his state of mind at this juncture. Buffett had been secretly distressed about his father's failing health due to cancer, but he managed his worry by immersing himself in work. His favourite work was of course to scout for good investments. In this scenario, he came across a textile company called Berkshire Hathaway, based in New Bedford, Massachusetts. Berkshire Hathaway's stock was available at a discount as the company was struggling to keep its business going. Though it had been a good business, the company had been closing mill after mill.

He slowly started accumulating the stock of Berkshire Hathaway, beginning 1962. He was aware that the president of the company, Seabury Stanton, was also buying. Buffett's plan was to keep buying as long as the price was cheap, and sell it back to the company when the price was satisfactorily high. To be careful, he bought through a broker, as he wanted to prevent people from knowing that he was interested. Buffett's skill had gained quite a reputation by then, and his association with the stock would have upped the price. Soon, Stanton got to know of Buffett's increasing purchases and he did not want to lose the ownership of the company. The two men met and Stanton agreed to buy from Buffett at the price of $11.50 per share, if there was a tender offer. There was a little detail though — this was merely an oral agreement. A few weeks later when Buffett got a letter from Berkshire Hathaway, the tender price had been mentioned as $11 and three-eighths. That was twelve and a half cents less than the oral agreement.

Buffett was furious, to say the least. Then, Buffett took a dramatic decision — he resolved to buy Berkshire Hathaway and fire Stanton, the man who had gone back on his word. Interestingly, Buffett himself had been in a habit of bargaining to fractions of dollars when buying stock. This time, he thought it was cheating on Stanton's part. He aggressively bought into the company and became the director. He then fired Stanton and gave charge to Ken Chace, a low-key employee of the same company whom Buffett had found to be honest and hardworking.

Getting ownership of this sick company became a sticky situation for Buffett. He had no use for a company that was day by day, failing to generate profit. He didn't understand much of textile business either. There was a lot of company assets to be disposed too. The smart thing would have been to liquidate the company. But Buffett did not want to be seen as a villain, a man who took away jobs of people, a feeling that he had had a brush with during the Dempster episode. So, he tried to run the textile company for a hard-to-believe 20 years.

At that time, he gave a public statement that he bought the company because he got it at a good price. Around five decades later, in an interview with CNBC, Buffett said that this was the most terrible business decision that he had made: 'The dumbest stock I ever bought – was – [drum] roll here – Berkshire Hathaway.'[10] He added, 'It was a terrible mistake, just because I drifted into it, in a sense.' Buffett had a word of advice from his experience: 'If you get in a lousy business, get out of it.'

It took him 20 years to close the business. Putting the resources into this company had cost him a loss of millions, and it hurt him to realize that if he had put that money into other investments, it would have grown manifold. The textile part of the business was closed in 1985.

Personal Loss

In 1964, Buffett's father was losing his battle with cancer. Even after many surgeries and treatments, there was little hope of him surviving the ordeal. He finally breathed his last on 30 April of that year. Warren Buffett had always revered his father. The period of Howard's illness itself had been a harrowing experience for Warren, but the death brought with it the toughest time for him. He handled the situation by immersing himself in work and more work.

Susan and Warren Buffett set up the Buffett Foundation with the purpose of donating to educational causes. Susan had always been a philanthropist at heart, and her influence was beginning to have an effect on Buffett's social and political approaches. Buffett, however, didn't think he had reached a stage of becoming a serious philanthropist. He still had long roads to travel before thinking of anything else.

Closing the Door of the Partnership

In 1965, Buffett closed BPL to more partners. The partnership had $44 million, but the market scenario was not particularly encouraging. There weren't many ideas for cigar butt investing. He told the partners that a further increase in the size of the partnership might be disadvantageous to the interests of the partners.

By the next year, the market scenario was grim. The market had plunged due to urban riots in different parts of the US. Mid-1966 also saw racial tensions and violence in Omaha and the National Guards had to be called in. The war with Vietnam was going on. There were anti-war protests in cities across the country. All this was not good news for the stock market.

Buffett knew that in this scenario, it won't be easy to find undervalued companies to be used as cigar butts. The American Express experience had set him thinking in the direction of acquiring whole companies, good ones, not sick ones like Berkshire.

Charlie Munger Joins Buffett

Munger and Buffett had been informally discussing their work without actually working with each other, but in January 1966, Buffett formed a company with Munger. There was also a third partner, David Gottesman. They named the company Diversified Retailing Company. The agenda was to acquire retail businesses and the first of these was Hochschild-Kohn, an American department store chain based in Baltimore, acquired for $12 million. Since the interest rates were not high, they got a loan sanctioned from a bank. This was the first time that Buffett had agreed to borrow a big amount of money, a fact that showed the increasing influence of Munger's way of functioning.

Bigger, diverse and more expensive prospects had started making their presence in Buffett's life, ushering in a new phase of life for him and his partners.

EXPANDING THE HORIZONS

Buffett was getting increasingly busy with work, but now he was looking towards different avenues, insurance being one of these. At the same time, he was beginning to get recognized as a brilliant money manager. However, he didn't publicize or talk to the media, wanting to stay away from the public eye. Yet, the first article about him appeared in the *Omaha World-Herald* in 1966. One of the reporters got interested in the talk about a young man who was bringing wonderful returns for his partners. The article ran the headline: 'Investor at 11, Warren Buffett Controls $45 Million Fund at 35'.[11] No one really imagined something impressive happening in the financial world in remote Omaha, far away from the financial capital of the country, but this was about Warren Buffett, who was to become famous, very famous, in the coming years.

Getting into Insurance: The Deal Made in Fifteen Minutes

It is often said that Buffett is so sharp at understanding businesses that he takes just a few minutes to decide whether to buy a company or not. The assumption might be true, given Buffett's passion for investments, his wide experience of dealing with hundreds of partners and studying thousands of pages of *Moody's* and *Standard and Poor's* manuals. Whether or not this is an overstatement, Buffett kept his eyes on whichever business he saw as a good prospect and continued studying it for some time before actually striking the deal.

Since 1967, Buffett was trying to put as little money into the Berkshire Hathaway textile business as possible. Instead, he was increasingly studying insurance companies and wanted to steer Berkshire in that direction. In his characteristic style, he studied all that he could lay his hands on to understand the insurance sector. The latter caught his attention because of the profitability it offered. It has a lucrative float: capital with no cost; there is a steady flow of premium; and the ratio of claims paid and the premiums collected lean heavily in the company's favour.

With these interests in mind, Buffett had been studying the Omaha-based National Indemnity Company, founded by Jack Ringwalt. Buffett was impressed with the efficiency of the management, primarily due to its leadership. The only problem was that Ringwalt wasn't interested in selling the company. Through a connection, Buffett came to know about a weird fact—for 15 minutes in a year, Ringwalt talked about selling the company. What this meant was that once in a while when Ringwalt would get into a bad mood and, for a small window of about 15 minutes, he would talk about selling his company. Strange as it may sound, people close to him knew about this rare time window when he could be convinced about selling National Indemnity. Buffett soon got a chance to access those 15 minutes. He didn't want to lose the opportunity, hence, going against his style of functioning, he accepted all the terms set by Ringwalt, even though he had to pay a price higher than what he had planned.

The deal was struck within an unbelievable 15 minutes! Ringwalt was probably taken aback, since he had never really wanted to sell his company. But he would not go back on his word. Buffett bought National

Indemnity through Berkshire Hathaway, not for BPL, for approximately $8.6 million. That turned out to be a great deal, as Buffett remarked decades later that if he hadn't done that, 'Berkshire would be lucky to be worth half of what it is today.'[12] This was just the beginning. Over the next few decades, Buffett would be owning positions in many more insurance companies.

Blue Chip Stamps

Buffett had found the 'float' lucrative in the insurance business. A similar prospect came to him in the form of a business called Blue Chip Stamps. These were coupon-like stamps that shoppers were given in proportion to the amount of money they spent on their purchases. The stamps could be redeemed later for purchase of merchandise like household goods. Buffett, along with Munger, got interested in this because the company had a float of around $90 million, due to the simple reason that there was a large time gap between selling the stamps to the stores and the time when customers redeemed them. The two men, along with a third partner, Rick Guerin, started buying shares of Blue Chip Stamps. Buffett invested through Berkshire and in 1969, the $2-million investment had grown into $7 million. The three partners slowly gained 60 per cent of the partnership of the company.

Owning a Bank

When Buffett came across information about the Illinois National Bank, also known as Rockford Bank, he figured out that this bank was extremely profitable. The prospect of owning a bank, and a profitable one at that, excited him, and he struck a deal. He later revealed that during this period, he observed that businessmen with strong ethics cared more about how the company would be treated by a new owner rather than how much money could be made out of the sale. This was precisely the attitude of Eugene Abegg, who agreed to sell to Buffett, even though the latter had quoted a price that was a million dollars less than another buyer's offer. Buffett immensely respected that.

Owning Newspapers

Buffett's childhood fascination with newspapers had created in him a deep-seated desire of owning a newspaper. Even though it didn't offer a lucrative business opportunity, he was increasingly becoming assertive about the need to have a social responsibility and he was aware of the role newspapers played in shaping information. Berkshire Hathaway bought the *Omaha Sun* newspaper in January 1969. In 1973, the newspaper won the most prestigious Pulitzer Prize for local investigative specialized reporting. Shortly after this, it bought a magazine—the *Washington Monthly*. It didn't do well.

In the 1970s, Buffett's ownership of a part of *The Washington Post* had a great influence on him as a person. Buffett had attained his deep-seated desire to have a place of influence in an important publishing establishment. This stake also introduced him to Katherine Graham, publisher of the paper, and the two became close friends. The association with Graham as well as with the board of directors introduced Buffett to the glittery world of Washington, with its high-profile people and parties. Buffett was of a different kind, but he found Washington interesting.

Buffett's passion for owning newspapers didn't end there. Over the next few decades, he built an entire empire, owning around 30 newspapers. Though he remained a staunch supporter of this domain throughout, in January 2020, Buffett announced that sadly, Berkshire Hathaway would be selling off its newspaper business. Buffett said that the business no longer sounded sustainable. Personally, though, the newspaper connection had come full circle for Buffett. From a paper boy, he had been the owner of many newspapers.

Closing Down Buffett Partnership, Ltd

When things are going exceptionally well for a businessperson, the tendency is to keep the ball rolling even if there are chances of the pace getting slower. Not for Buffett, though. This was a man who would keep his integrity above everything else.

In 1969, he took the momentous decision of dissolving the partnership, BPL. It was a shocker to the partners, and most of them didn't want that to happen. For more than a decade, Buffett had been growing their money at a rate that was many times what it could grow if invested elsewhere, a compounded annual rate of 30 per cent before fees. The annual return on investment at the Dow was just around 7 per cent for this duration. Buffett had continuously surpassed his own projections and had never brought in a loss. The partners had come to regard him with awe. On his part, Buffett too had become attached to his partners. Though his job did not require it, he went to great lengths to give suggestions and recommendations to them on how to proceed further.

His reasons to close the partnership were complicated, though. The market scenario had been changing for the last few years. Buffett felt that he could no longer do business the way he had been doing it. Though he did not feel out of place in the changing market, he felt he would be able to get only mediocre results, since his old approach might not work and the partners' money would be at stake. He had often repeated that the partners shared a common set of values with him, hence, to him, they were like family. He was not ready to put his partners' money into a risky zone, hence, in a great act of honesty, he told them the truth. The episode remains as an extraordinary act of integrity on Buffett's part.

At the closure of the partnership, Buffett and his wife together had an ownership of 36 per cent in Berkshire, 13 per cent of Blue Chip and 39 per cent in Diversified

Retailing Company. Buffett named himself chairman of Berkshire Hathaway. The company was moving further from its primary identity of a textile business, and a new phase in Buffett's life began, the phase of the great shift from cigar butts to having 'wonderful companies'.

NO STOPPING:
TOWARDS THE ZENITH

Buffett had come far from the dreamy days when as a child, he had set a goal of becoming a millionaire. He had been continuously pulling the goal post towards himself, achieving every goal before the deadline he has set for himself. Now, he was moving in the direction of becoming a multi-billionaire. He had been working towards dissolving DRC and Blue Chip Stamps, and devoting himself entirely to Berkshire Hathaway. Berkshire Hathaway functioned as a holding company, but the strategy now was of buying 'wonderful companies at a fair price', something that Buffett had started learning from Munger even before the latter joined as vice chairman of Berkshire Hathaway in 1978.

Wonderful Companies at a Fair Price

One of the earliest such deals came in the form of See's Candies. The company wanted to sell for $30 million, when it had assets of only $5 million. The price, it said, was for the reputation of the brand, as it had earned the much-coveted customer goodwill. Before Munger's influence had begun to show, Buffett perhaps wouldn't have gone ahead with such an overpriced commodity. Now, since he had opened himself up to larger investments, he could easily figure out that a business such as a good-quality confectionary that had a respectable market presence would definitely turn out to be a good investment. He was looking at the long-term profit of owning such a business. It did turn out to be a hugely profitable investment, earning over $2 billion till 2019. With this deal, Buffett had graduated to the big league of buying companies at a 'fair price'.

View from the Top

The journey after that is a jaw-dropping story of incredible growth. Buffett was fast on his way to becoming one of the richest men in the world. For over five decades, Buffett has been ceaselessly doing what he loves to do the most—invest. The acquisitions grew bigger with each passing year and currently, Berkshire Hathaway owns, wholly or partly, the biggest names in the business world. The focus, as always, has remained on long-term investments. Both Buffett and Munger were particular about staying away from the kind of speculative investing everyone was doing. They instead focused on stable businesses with reasonably predictable long-term growth.

Over time, his Berkshire Hathaway acquired dozens of companies that includes insurance companies; notable among those is GEICO. Buffett had a keen interest in this stock since his college days and in 1996, he acquired the company. Berkshire also has an extraordinary achievement in the insurance sector in the US in the form of Berkshire Hathaway Assurance that insures municipal and local government bonds. Buffett's and Munger's strong commitment to ethics ensured that all of Berkshire Hathaway's insurance concerns are rated AAA by Standard and Poor's Corporation, the highest authority in financial rating. The company also has an A++ rating for their operating performance and financial situation. This rating is provided by A.M. Best, the American credit rating agency.

CEO Warren Buffett's untiring work through decades led to Berkshire Hathaway becoming one of the largest public companies in the world and was the largest financial services company by revenue according to Forbes Global list of 2020. From a stock price of $300 in 1980, in 2020, it held the record for having the costliest share price in history, with its Class-A shares trading at a whopping $300,000 each. The reason is that Buffett was determined never to split Class-A shares of the company. Consequently, the price was never broken up. In classic Warren Buffett style, the decision not to split was a deliberate attempt to keep those people away who might want to trade this stock to make a quick buck. Buffett has always wanted to treat his partners as family, and that is a long-term commitment. 'Buffett has always viewed Berkshire's shareholders as partners in the business, rather than just investors in a large public company. He wants them to stick around and to stay invested.'[13]

However, Buffett realized that having only Class-A shares might bring in investors like unit trusts or mutual funds who might sell pieces of Class-A shares for a profit. He saw this as a threat as the dealers might appear to be Berkshire Hathaway lookalikes. They could have charged high fees and the investors might have come out unhappy. Buffett has always been obsessed with keeping the investors happy. So, to avoid such a situation, in 1996, Class-B shares were introduced that could be bought at a much cheaper price, but with 1/1,000th of the voting rights of Class-A shares.

Berkshire Hathaway also owns scores of other businesses, which include energy corporations, railroads, manufacturing companies, retail chains, clothing lines, media houses and real estate. It also wholly owns big names in the US market such as the chain of fast-food restaurants Dairy Queen, the garment maker Fruit of the Loom and the popular battery maker Duracell. Besides, it has an equity stake in many big names across the globe, but five of these account for around 65 per cent of Berkshire Hathaway's portfolio. These are Apple Inc., The Coca Cola Company, IBM, American Express, and Wells Fargo and Company.

At the age of 55, Buffett became a billionaire, ranked among 14 billionaires in the US by *Forbes*. In 2008, with a net worth of $62 billion, he became the richest person in the world, and he continues to rank among the richest people of the world till date. It was not just a growth in his personal wealth. For the first time, a money manager, a person who helped people grow their wealth, had achieved this feat. By the late 1980s, Berkshire Hathaway's book value had seen a growth of more than 20 per cent a year, that too for around 23 years. One thousand dollars invested into the partnership at the beginning were worth $1.1 million. Those figures continued to grow astronomically. Ten thousand dollars invested at the start of the partnership swelled to $240 million in 2017. The names Buffett or Berkshire have become synonymous with spectacular financial statistics. Remarkably, Buffett remains exceptionally down to earth in describing his exploits, as if it was a routine, humble activity.

The Oracle of Everything

Buffett's uncanny ability to identify good stocks not only made people wide-eyed, but also earned him an exclusive title: The Oracle of Omaha. Just like an oracle, Buffett seemed to have some supernatural powers to point out stocks that could lead to exceptional results. He had attained an almost superhuman status, and his words were followed like the scriptures. CNN Money has nicely captured the essence when it says that Buffett was right not just about the stocks, but also about accounting, CEO functioning and corporate governance.[14]

'For decades, the name Warren Buffett has conjured up the image of a golden-touch investor — a solid, straight-shooting, deep value-minded soul who (as dozens of biographies and investing primers will tell you) believes in buying "companies", not stocks. His effect on the stock market rivals that of Federal Reserve chairmen and US presidents; his investing style is studied and copied by legions of acolytes from Wall Street to small-town America; his missives in Berkshire Hathaway's annual reports are read (and cited) as if they were the Gospel itself.'[15]

Buffett's extraordinary understanding of the market had led to certain equally extraordinary situations. It is said that Buffett almost predicted the financial crisis of 2008. Even if prediction is an overstatement, he did warn that mortgage derivatives in the housing market could spell a potential disaster. His words came true when the US financial system was on the verge of collapsing due to the mentioned factor.

In a dramatic situation, in the midst of the financial crisis, Buffett called up the treasury secretary in the then president George Bush's administration, and gave advice on how to save the economy.[16] It turned out to be the basic idea on which the administration worked and bailed out the ailing banks. The Oracle of Omaha justified the title ascribed to him.

Some Mistakes and Regrets

Buffett had always felt comfortable buying businesses that he says he 'understands'. If he doesn't feel comfortable about a business, he avoids buying it. As a result, he regrets missing a few opportunities, among which is not investing in Google. Even though the founders of Google, Larry Page and Sergey Brin, visited Buffett in the 2000s, the latter decided against investing in the company. Later, however, he said that he regrets the decision. 'It was and is an extraordinary business and it has some aspects of a natural monopoly… It's great to find something that costs a penny and sells for a dollar and is habit forming.' He added saying, 'We blew it.'[17]

A more serious trouble came to him in the form of an investment in Salomon Brothers. Buffett made an investment of $700 million in the company, but in 1991, a scandal was unearthed. An investigation was launched into the scandalous trading of treasury bonds, once even buying bonds in the name of a fictitious customer. Buffett's reputation, gathered over the years, was at stake. As the company was banned by the treasury, Buffett stepped in to save the day. He ran the business for a few months and pulled it out of the situation.

As billionaire Buffett got more and more involved with big money, his image became synonymous with money, piles of money, a genius who is always thinking right and getting richer. It is often ignored that behind those stacks of dollar bills is a human, a son, a husband, a father, a man with emotions.

THE LIFE AND THE EMPIRE WARREN BUFFETT BUILT

The Secret to Buffett's Magic

There can be no magic mantra to achieve success. It is invariably a combination of various factors. Buffett has shared his wisdom with the world numerous times, and he describes his tremendous accomplishments in such simple words that it sounds like cakewalk. It is no secret that rarely is anyone so astoundingly and so consistently successful as he is. The endless hours of calculation, observation, sweat and toil seem to become almost invisible when one sees the Warren Buffett of today. The apparently smooth journey to the top had serious challenges. Above all, it required certain qualities in a person, and Buffett had them in abundance. What he has achieved is a delicate mixture of personal qualities and persistent hard work.

Personal Qualities

Buffett's ability to focus on a topic is legendary. He never let the target go out of sight, but just desiring a goal is one thing and toiling towards it is altogether another level. He is a voracious reader since his childhood and is known to read around eight hours a day. His patience is equally well-known, whether it be in stocks or in personal relationships. Being patient in the stock market has given him handsome returns repeatedly. Another remarkable thing about him is his self-discipline. Buffett always liked to be systematic, and was not diverted from his tasks, even while working from home in the early days of his business. While giving advice to young people, he often mentions the skill of public speaking. This isn't surprising, since he himself saw a sea change in his life by gaining this one skill.

Do What You Love

Buffett insists that if people find jobs that they would like to do when they don't need a job, they are sure to be successful. He says that even while nearing 90 years of age, he still springs up from bed and 'tap dances to work'. He is working at an age when most people would have retired two decades ago. With the amount of money he has, he doesn't need to work, but with the amount of love he has for his work, there can be no stopping.

Free Thinking

Buffett chose to work away from the happening stock exchange at New York. He didn't think it necessary to be in a certain place to find good companies to invest in. He only thought it essential to study the financial statements of the companies concerned and work from a place that he felt comfortable in. In many other aspects of his life, he followed the same thing. He never tried to dress in a certain way that society expected or to have houses and cars that people associate with mega-billionaires. The same applied to his choice of stocks. 'Mr Market' was never successful in influencing his decisions.

The Empire

Buffett's office, the headquarters at Kiewit Plaza in Omaha, reportedly has a staff of just around 25 people. The office does not have the form expected of any large organization. However, Buffett's business associates include thousands of shareholders, who congregate at the annual shareholders meeting. The environment is that of a grand festival, even a pilgrimage, for students of investing. An interesting aspect of this event is that Buffett and Munger participate in a marathon session of questions and answers, which sometimes goes up to five hours. The event has been aptly nicknamed 'Woodstock for Capitalists'.

One unique feature of Buffett's way of working is his annual letters to shareholders. He has been writing these open letters to the shareholders for over 40 years. He often infuses wit and a hint of his teaching into these letters. These letters have attained the status of archetypal texts that provide a peek into this genius's mind. The letters have become a must-read for investors and are eagerly awaited every year.

Rules for Investing

Buffett says there are only two rules for investing. Rule number one: never lose money; rule number two: never forget rule number one. To make a complicated thing sound so simple, only Warren Buffett can do it.

His witty remarks aside, he has a few practical guidelines for investors. The first of these is what he calls his **'circle of competence'**: buy what you understand. Buffett bought only those businesses which he said he could understand. As the teacher that he loves to be, Buffett explains that 'understanding' does not refer to delving into the details of how the business is done, for example, understanding how dresses are made in a garment factory. Instead, the reference is to having a clear view of the financial health of the company, to be able to see where the company would be heading in the coming years.

To this, Buffett adds that there is no need for anyone to go out and have expertise in a number of things. Finding one's area of interest and competence is the key. This brings us to his other rule: **do what you like.** He asserts that a person would succeed if he makes a career in his area of interest, suggesting that it is important to identify the work that would make one truly happy rather than the one that is trending in the market. The reason is logical — people would give more than their 100 per cent if they are passionate about their jobs.

Buffett also insists on buying shares for their value, not for their market price. He suggests that an investor should look at the **long-term value** of the stock, not short-term gains. Staying away from risky investments is another of his suggestions. Risk, he says, comes from not understanding the business one is investing in. **Patience**, again, pays in the long run, so investors should look for stock they can hold on for years and be happy. That comes from carefully researching and understanding a business before investing in it.

Having a 'moat' around the business is another of Buffett's famous expressions. In common terminology, a moat is a protective trench dug around a castle or a fort, which is filled with water so that if the enemy attacks, it cannot easily access the building. The moat around a business actually means a competitive advantage over a long term. Businesses that typically are dependent on one leader or specialist, don't have a moat around them.

He thinks Coca-Cola is one example of a company with that moat.

Some Failures and Setbacks

Besides mentioning that buying Berkshire Hathaway (the original company) was his biggest mistake, Buffett has had a few other misses too. He did not buy a stake in Amazon and Google in the early days. The interesting thing is that Buffett admires the Amazon business and says that it has achieved close to a 'miracle', but that is also the reason why he had stayed away from the super business for long. In the early days, he bought businesses like Dexter Shoe Co., which turned out to be a 'financial disaster'. Even after the failed effort to revive the Berkshire textile mills, Buffett bought another textile company more than a decade after that. The Waumbec Textile Company proved to be another mistake.

What makes Buffett the legend that he is is the fact that his mistakes did not deter him. His unending thirst for learning led him to learn from each of his mistakes. Instead of giving up after the mistakes, he carefully analysed and understood the situations and then directed all his energy towards the next goal.

He has also suffered a serious health problem when in 2012 he was diagnosed with stage one prostate cancer. He was treated with radiation therapy, but what is most remarkable is the way he communicated the news to the world. His tone was cheery and the words were the lightest possible. He said that the cancer was not a big deal and was not life-threatening at all. After the treatment, he said he felt 'terrific', and like a man intensely in love with his work, which he definitely is, he added that the treatment did not require him to take a day off work. Buffett cannot be easily diverted from the love of his life, even by a health condition — that is the extent of his passion towards his work.

The Unique Leader

Buffett believes it won't make any sense to own good businesses if the managers running those businesses are not good. Buffett and Berkshire Hathaway never interfere in the work of the management of the businesses they own. Berkshire's interference is miniscule; the advice it gives is limited to its area of specialization. The concept sounds simple but is a bit tricky to implement. Buffett believes in finding good managers and then leaving the job to them. He looks not just for capability in the person but also for integrity. A manager who keeps his shareholders' interest above his own ego or personal interest is a worthwhile candidate to him. Buffett has great respect for the managers and the CEOs running successful businesses, and acknowledges that they are great leaders and they know their job. As for his own concern, Berkshire, he says that he has wonderful people working with him, but it is very important to envision future goals. Even more important, he stresses, is to make his team understand that vision. Much loved and respected as Buffett is, his leadership style is considered exemplary.

Buffett has constantly taken ownership of his partners' and shareholders' interests above other things. In the late 1990s, he was being criticized for denying his partners a big share of profit by not investing in technology companies. Buffett was clear-headed. He did not want to invest his partners' money in things he did not understand. His sense of responsibility is prominent, and at the same time, his humility is disarming. Like an inspirational leader, he admits his mistakes openly. But Buffett doesn't stop at that; he analyses how the mistakes could have been avoided or amended. That gives his observers a wealth of knowledge to apply in their own lives. Another quality that makes him almost superhuman is that he is not swayed by public opinion. He has always been his own guide, a trailblazer in the world of investing.

BEHsIND THE PILES OF MONEY

At the pinnacle of success, Buffett has reached an iconic status. He is deified as the unquestionable lord of investing. However, behind all those piles of money and oodles of fame, there is a human being who has had his share of insecurities; who has suffered personal, devastating losses; who fell madly in love; who has made mistakes; who has a childlike preference for certain things.

The Beautiful but Unusual Love Story

The name Warren Buffett is all about money, but only to the outside world. As an individual, he had the most moving experience in life when he fell in love. Buffett's love story began as a fairy tale but transformed into a delicate tale of unusual complexity, yet retaining its beauty. As a young man, Buffett wasn't particularly good with girls, mostly due to his lack of confidence with public speaking. As he gained that skill and dated a few girls, the confidence grew, and he finally got Susan as his wife, the girl whom he had been fixated on for a long time. The timing to learn public speaking couldn't have been better. He did actually win over another suitor that Susan was dating. Once married, Warren and Susan Buffett were madly in love, always taking care to keep each other happy.

As Buffett grew busier with his work, Susan practically handled everything concerning her home, kids, in-laws, friends and extended family. She was a perpetual source of comfort and emotional security for her husband. Buffett has remarked more than once that it was because of Susan that he was able to accomplish so much, going as far as to mention her as one of his heroes — his father and Ben Graham being the other two.

When Susan and Warren Buffett started a family, the latter was always there for his family physically, but his mind was elsewhere — in his work. Though the family had meals together, went on vacations and were together in everything like a normal family, Susan found her husband to be mentally distant, but she understood.

As much as Buffett was interested in making huge amounts of money, Susan was not interested in money at all. Both were on the same page in believing that when they would have a great amount of money, they would give back to society. The two had formed the Buffett Foundation in 1964, of which Susan was the president. Complexity arose when Susan wanted to give money through charity, help or foundations pretty early. She was always a most helpful person, going out of her way to do things even for strangers. Her interest in money was much inclined towards what it could do to help less privileged people. Buffett, on the other hand, wanted to reach a certain level before he would give away. At the same time, he never restrained her from using money the way she wanted to.

As their children grew up, Susan's inclination for social work increased as she now had more time to spend with organizations in which she was involved as an activist for civil rights, abortion and birth control rights. Buffett was so busy, having reached the peak of his career that he could not participate in every activity of her interest. She began to feel as if she needed to find an identity of her own, and with the amount of money she had, she could be doing something worthwhile for society. Buffett was reportedly briefly attracted towards Katherine Graham, publisher of the *Washington Post*. Overall, though, Warren and Susan loved each other and got along nicely.

It was an extraordinary decision when Susan decided to leave Omaha to pursue a singing career. She did not leave her husband, though. They never got divorced. She told a devastated Warren that she would be there for him always and would join him whenever he wanted, but she needed to go live in San Francisco. He was shell-shocked at first, and wondered if he did not have the skill to understand people. Gradually, he accepted the situation. The two continued meeting whenever possible and making appearances at annual meetings as a couple.

A strange twist came to the story when Susan, upon leaving Omaha, asked one of her friends to take care of Buffett. She was Astrid Menks, a former restaurant hostess. Menks moved in with Buffett and the two became companions. Strangely, the arrangement suited all, including the Buffett's three children. They liked Menks a lot. It is said that Christmas cards from the Buffett household had three names undersigned:

Warren, Susan and Astrid. This unusual arrangement suited the entire family and Menks was loved by all.

Warren Buffett faced the toughest time of his life when Susan was diagnosed with oral cancer. Despite a surgery and a painful treatment time, she died of a heart stroke in 2004. The arrangements in the couple's life were strange, but the love hadn't faded. Buffett went into a seriously low phase of his life after Susan's death. Two years after Susan's death, Menks and Buffett got married in 2006, when the latter was 76 years of age. Buffett has a word of caution: this unusual arrangement worked fine for him but might not work for other people.

The Father

Even though Buffett was not like the modern, hands-on fathers, his three children felt loved and are attached to their father. Growing up, they knew that their father was always busy with some 'big stuff', but none of them were made to feel that they were growing up in a rich household. They didn't know that their father was rich or famous. Like the other kids, they did chores and got allowances. The three children were probably unaware of the great effort Warren and Susan were putting into making this happen. The two tried to give their children a normal childhood, without making them feel privileged. They felt it was important in order to have their children grow up to be independent individuals who would make their own lives. Buffett was also particular about teaching financial responsibility to his kids. Their eldest child, Susan, has carried forward the good work of her mother, working on a number of social causes as a philanthropist. Howard, the second child, has been a politician, a businessman, a photographer and a philanthropist. The youngest, Peter, is a musician, author and philanthropist.

Although Warren Buffett's net worth is more than $85 billion in the beginning of 2020, he plans not to leave most of his money to his children. He is satisfied with giving them $2 billion each, but having signed the 'Giving Pledge', 99 per cent of his wealth will go towards charitable causes. The reason for not leaving his inheritance to his children is interesting. He says that he wants to leave his kids 'enough money so that they would feel they could do anything, but not so much that they could do nothing'.[18]

The Philanthropist

Susan and Warren had formed the Buffett Foundation, and Susan had been doing charitable work through her life. Warren Buffett has donated millions to the Bill and Melinda Gates Foundation and to the philanthropic organizations run by his three children. But the most noticeable philanthropic event in Buffett's life is the 'Giving Pledge'. He co-founded it with Bill and Melinda Gates in 2006. Buffett has pledged to donate more than 99 per cent of his wealth during his lifetime or at death. Till this time, Buffett had been criticized of sitting on piles of money without giving any of it away. It was actually not in popular knowledge that the Buffett Foundation, later renamed Susan Thompson Buffett Foundation, had been donating millions to charitable causes, in addition to donating $134 million to unspecified charities in 1999. Also, he had been giving $5 million per annum to the Nuclear Threat Initiative. He was still accused of holding back a lot of money. When he donated to the Bill and Melinda Gates Foundation, questions were raised again about why he was entrusting it to the Microsoft founder than doing it himself. Buffett had a simple reply. He said that when there are people around who have expertise in the area and when he trusts their intention and capability, why would he make an effort of doing it himself? It was, he said, not his skill. Personally, all through his life, he had been hoping that one day this task would be done by Susan, but after her death, he delegated the task to the people he trusted.

With the Giving Pledge, in one stroke he had promised to give most of his wealth away. His reasons for doing so are not just interesting; they have a rare, heart-warming quality. The reasons are explained in his letter for the Giving Pledge, in his characteristic simple, easy-to-understand style. The most touching of the lines would be engraved in people's memories for a long time:

More than 99% of my wealth will go to philanthropy during my lifetime or at death. Measured by dollars, this commitment is large. In a comparative sense, though, many individuals give more to others every day… Millions of people who regularly contribute to churches, schools, and other organizations thereby relinquish the use of funds that would otherwise benefit their own families. The dollars these people drop into a collection plate or give to United Way mean forgone movies, dinners out, or other personal pleasures. In contrast, my family and I will give up nothing we need or want by fulfilling this 99% pledge…Were we to use more than 1% of my claim checks (Berkshire Hathaway stock certificates) on ourselves, neither our happiness nor our well-being would be enhanced. In contrast, that remaining 99% can have a huge effect on the health and welfare of others.[19]

To answer why he waited for so long to give away the money, Buffett has a classic answer that is sure to disarm even a sceptic listener. He says that he figured out early that he was good at compounding money. He had a mutual understanding with his wife that they would give away most of their money, but he wanted to let the pile grow substantially before he did that. The logic was simple: when he had the ability to donate billions, why should be donate mere millions?

In the Hall of Fame of Thriftiness

Closely related to his criticism about sitting on cash is his famous habit of living a frugal life. He is considered as one of the most frugal mega-billionaires ever. Many stories revolve around this habit of his. He still lives in the modest house he bought in 1958 and drives a simple car. He doesn't really dress up in expensive clothes. He didn't use a smartphone until recently. He doesn't use a credit card, though he has an old American Express credit card. He has McDonald's breakfast, and remembers, down to the cents, the price of each meal he buys. He is famous for not spending a penny extra on anything. The one thing that he has splurged his money on is a private jet.

His reasons for his apparent thriftiness are a lesson in practicality. He simply does not believe in possessing things for the sake of demonstrating his wealth. 'Some material things make my life more enjoyable; many, however, would not. I like having an expensive private plane, but owning a half-dozen homes would be a burden. Too often, a vast collection of possessions ends up possessing its owner.'[20] Understanding the fine line between possessing wealth and the wealth possessing a person shows a remarkable level of elevated thought process, which surely cannot be present in a man driven by pure greed.

Political Views

Buffett always revered his father and was offended when his father was criticized for his ideological approach. His relation with his father was not just respectful; it was a deep emotional bond too. In the famous 2017 BBC documentary on Warren Buffett, an interviewer asks him if he remembered his father's last words. Buffett's eyes turn unmistakably sad just as he tries to smile bravely and answers in a tone of anguish, 'Yeah, but I don't want to talk about it.'[21]

It was hence obvious that a change in his political inclination would lead Buffett to a dilemma. Howard Buffett being a Republican congressman, Warren had naturally grown up with the Republican thought process. However, after getting married to Susan, Warren became increasingly aware of the necessity for the civil rights movement. Susan was an active participant in the civil rights and often made friends with people of other races. To reinforce her ideas of equality, she went out of her way to help them. Buffett too had been widening his circle to get equal rights for all, including people of African origin and Jews since his Columbia days. The iconic speech by Martin Luther King Jr had a huge impact on him.

Gradually, Buffett's liberal views became clearer and he found himself more inclined towards the Democrats. He would never have wanted to hurt his father by telling him about his drastically changed political affiliation. He felt relieved that his active participation in Democratic politics happened only after his father's death. He is not unhappy about his earlier Republican affiliation, though. He feels that different times warrant different things and it is okay to change with the changing environments.

Buffett went on to get actively involved in politics in various ways. He has supported liberal candidates both financially and in the form of endorsement. He lent his support to Barack Obama as well as to Hillary Clinton.

Warren Buffett Equals Junk Food?

At 90 years of age, Buffett is a powerhouse of energy. Shattering all concepts of 'healthy eating' for a longer life and boundless energy is the truth about his eating habits. His diet is made mostly of junk food high on sugar and salt. He stays at an arm's length from vegetables. It is rumoured that he doesn't ever drink water. Buffett once remarked that he is one quarter Coca-Cola. Always a human calculator, Buffett says that he consumes a consistent 2,700 calories in a day, out of which one-fourth comes from the Coca-Cola he drinks.

He often has his breakfast from McDonald's and once even took his friend Bill Gates for a meeting to a McDonald's. Buffett loves candies and ice cream, and that explains his childlike joy at buying See's Candies and Dairy Queen, a joy that is still reflected on his face when he talks about the long-term value of these businesses. Once when his doctor advised him to choose between eating better and exercising, he chose the latter, which he called the lesser of the two evils. He's often joked that he would be willing to give up a year of his life in exchange of not eating things like broccoli and asparagus.

Well, all the speculation apart, a sharp genius as Warren Buffett wouldn't be taking chances with his health, particularly since he loves the idea of having a long life. That brings in an interesting aspect: Buffett for sure has a knack of figuring out what works for him. And it works for him just fine, though it would be wrong to see it as an ideal diet.

Friends

Buffett's advice to young people mentions among other things, the need to have valuable friends in one's life. The reason he says is that people better than you would push you in a direction that is going to be fruitful for you. Buffett has always treated his partners as family, but two of his friends are remarkable. The first is Charlie Munger. Buffett and Munger are de facto mascots for Berkshire Hathaway, with their caricatures decorating innumerable spaces, even merchandise. The two say that they had never had an argument in 60 years of their friendship, though they often had huge disagreements.

Another of Buffett's famous friends is Microsoft founder Bill Gates. Interestingly, Gates initially didn't want to meet Buffett as he was sceptical about a stock market person, while his own interest was in inventing things. When Gates's parents asked him to join them at a dinner meeting where Buffett was a guest, Gates tried to excuse himself, but eventually joined. He had no idea that from the very first meeting, he would get along so well with Buffett. The association quickly blossomed into a strong friendship. This is in spite of Buffett having close to zero interest in computers; he doesn't even have a computer in his office.

Painting His Own Painting

Buffett's life is a story of inspirational focus, discipline, self-belief, hard work and, above all, ethics. From the young man who wanted to be a millionaire someday to one of the richest, most powerful and revered investors of all times, his journey has been incredibly inspiring. Though it took him an unbelievable amount of hard work to get to this station in life, he is extremely humble about it.

He also downplays the accolades awarded to his profession, almost lamenting that many other valuable professions are unfortunately not given high rewards in our world: 'I've worked in an economy that rewards someone who saves the lives of others on a battlefield with a medal, rewards a great teacher with thank-you notes from parents, but rewards those who can detect the mispricing of securities with sums reaching into the billions. In short, fate's distribution of long straws is wildly capricious.'[22]

There are and will be many things said and written about Warren Buffett, but one thing stands out: his love for his work. It is no mean feat to be excited every day about going to work at the age of 90. That is because he has been enjoying 'painting his own painting'. Buffett himself has aptly described it in a speech. 'I get to paint my own painting. I go down there every day and I feel like Michelangelo working on the Sistine Chapel or something. Nobody else may think it's a great painting, but I get to paint my own painting.'[23]

In creating his own work of art, Buffett has given a precious gift to the world. He has crafted an extraordinary legend that is going to inspire millions of people for decades to come, for this has been the tale of a man who never compromised on his principles, yet built an unbelievable fortune not just for himself, but for others too.

REFERENCES

1. Alice Schroeder, *The Snowball: Warren Buffett and the Business of Life*, Bantam Books, 2009.
2. Warren Buffett - HBO Documentary HD, https://www.youtube.com/watch?v=RYHPlLsdW0A, accessed 23 February 2021.
3. ibid.
4. Phil Town, 'How to invest: Margin of safety—The growth rate', *Rule One Investing*, https://www.ruleoneinvesting.com/blog/how-to-invest/how-to-invest-margin-of-safety-the-growth-rate/, accessd 23 February 2021.
5. Gillian Zoe Segal, 'Billionaire Warren Buffett: "This $100 college course gave me the most important degree I have"—and it's why I'm successful today,' CNBC Make it, 21 March 2019, https://www.cnbc.com/2019/03/21/billionaire-warren-buffett-says-a-100-dollar-course-had-the-biggest-impact-on-his-success.html, accessed 10 February 2021.

6. Alice Schroeder, *The Snowball: Warren Buffett and the Business of Life*, Bantam Books, 2009.

7. Kathleen Elkins and Zameena Mejia, 'Warren Buffett credits his success to these 3 people,' CNBC Make It, 29 September 2017, https://www.cnbc.com/2017/09/29/warren-buffett-credits-his-success-to-these-3-people.html, accessed 10 February 2021.

8. Nathaniel Lee, 'Warren Buffett lives in a modest house that's worth .001% of his total wealth,' *Business Insider*, 10 November 2020, https://www.businessinsider.com/warren-buffett-modest-home-bought-31500-looks-2017-6?IR=T, accessed 10 February 2021.

9. Steve Jordon, 'Warren Buffett and Charlie Munger: Billion-dollar partnership,' *Omaha World-Herld*, 2 May 2015, https://www.omaha.com/money/buffett/warren-buffett-and-charlie-munger-billion-dollar-partnership/article_2819b16e-1933-51a7-b14b-002d9bb918de.html, accessed 10 February 2021.

10. Alex Crippen, 'CNBC Transcript: Warren Buffett's $200B Berkshire Blunder and the Valuable Lesson He Learned,' CNBC, 18 October 2010, https://www.cnbc.com/id/39724884, accessed 11 February 2021.

11. Steve Jordan, As Buffett's fortune rose, so did his fame,' *World-Herald*, 8 December 2013, https://www.omaha.com/news/as-buffett-s-fortune-rose-so-did-his-fame/article_b558c5e9-b4e3-5129-b8f9-bf1429a24bc5.html, accessed 11 February 2021.

12. Matthew Frankel, 'Warren Buffett and the Insurance Business: A 52-Year Love Story,' yahoo! Finance, 22 February 2019, https://in.finance.yahoo.com/news/warren-buffett-insurance-business-52-114100246.html, accessed 11 February 2021.

13. John Szramiak, 'Berkshire Hathaway's stock isn't that expensive,' *Insider*, 13 April 2016, https://www.businessinsider.com/berkshire-hathaways-stock-not-expensive-2016-4?IR=T, accessed 11 February 2021.

14. Andy Serwer and Julia Boorstin, 'The oracle of everything Warren Buffett has been right about the stock market, rotten accounting, CEO greed, and corporate governance. The rest of us are just catching on,' CNN Money, 11 November 2002, https://money.cnn.com/magazines/fortune/fortune_archive/2002/11/11/331843/index.htm, accessed 11 February 2021.

15. ibid.

16. Theron Mohamed, 'Warren Buffett phoned Treasury Secretary Hank Paulson with a stimulus idea when the 2008 financial crisis erupted,' *Business Insider India*, 11 October 2020, https://www.businessinsider.in/stock-market/news/warren-buffett-phoned-treasury-secretary-hank-paulson-with-a-stimulus-idea-when-the-financial-crisis-erupted-it-may-have-saved-the-us-economy/articleshow/78602664.cms, accessed 11 February 2021.

17. Theron Mohamed, '"We blew it": Warren Buffett admitted he messed up by not investing in Google,' *Markets Insider*,

27 January 2020, https://markets.businessinsider.com/news/stocks/warren-buffett-berkshire-hathaway-blew-it-not-investing-google-stock-2020-1-1028845920, accessed 11 February 2021.

18. Emmie Martin, '7 Billionaires Who Won't Leave Their Fortunes to Their Kids,' CNBC Make it, 6 July 2017, https://www.cnbc.com/2017/07/06/billionaires-who-wont-leave-their-fortunes-to-their-kids.html, accessed 12 February 2021.

19. Warren Buffett, 'My Philanthropic Pledge', *The Giving Pledge*, https://givingpledge.org/Pledger.aspx?id=177, accessed 12 February 2021.

20. ibid.

21. Doc Film BBC, 'Documentary Film Warren Buffett—BBC Documentary 2017', YouTube, 16 August 2017, https://www.youtube.com/watch?v=fvn77sw-vZg.

22. Warren Buffett, 'My Philanthropic Pledge', *The Giving Pledge*, https://givingpledge.org/Pledger.aspx?id=177, accessed 12 February 2021.

23. Warren Buffett, 'Warren Buffett on Painting His Own Painting...', *Value Investing World*, 3 April 2018, https://www.valueinvestingworld.com/2018/04/warren-buffett-on-painting-his-own.html, accessed 12 February 2021.